English Reading
for Academic Purposes

A Course Book for Graduate Students
of Science and Technology

研究生学术英语阅读

理工类

ENGLISH

总主编 陈新仁 黄 燕

主 编 刘长江 饶 辉

副主编 王秀文

编 者 刘长江 饶 辉

王秀文 李 迟

曹 华

清华大学出版社

北 京

内 容 简 介

《研究生学术英语阅读：理工类》是“研究生学术英语实用教程”系列教材之一。本教材基于学生对英语学术文献阅读的现实需求，全方位呈现学术英语文体尤其是理工类学术论文的篇章结构特征和语言特点，旨在培养学生的通用学术英语文本阅读技能及写作技能。与同类教材相比，本教材更具系统性和可操作性，支持研究型学习，可以满足研究生以及高年级本科生快速、有效提升学术英语阅读能力的需求。

本教材另配有练习的答案详解，读者可登录 ftp://ftp.tup.tsinghua.edu.cn/ 下载使用。

图书在版编目（CIP）数据

研究生学术英语阅读：理工类 / 陈新仁，黄燕总主编；刘长江，饶辉主编 . —北京：清华大学出版社，2022.6

ISBN 978-7-302-60917-9

Ⅰ. ①研… Ⅱ. ①陈… ②黄… ③刘… ④饶… Ⅲ. ①英语—阅读教学—研究生—教材 Ⅳ. ① H319.4

中国版本图书馆 CIP 数据核字（2022）第 088664 号

责任编辑：刘细珍
封面设计：李尘工作室
责任校对：王凤芝
责任印制：杨 艳

出版发行：清华大学出版社
网 址：http://www.tup.com.cn, http://www.wqbook.com
地 址：北京清华大学学研大厦 A 座 **邮 编：**100084
社 总 机：010-83470000 **邮 购：**010-62786544
投稿与读者服务：010-62776969, c-service@tup.tsinghua.edu.cn
质量反馈：010-62772015, zhiliang@tup.tsinghua.edu.cn
印 装 者：大厂回族自治县彩虹印刷有限公司
经 销：全国新华书店
开 本：185mm×260mm **印 张：**13 **字 数：**249 千字
版 次：2022 年 8 月第 1 版 **印 次：**2022 年 8 月第 1 次印刷
定 价：59.00 元

产品编号：095241-01

总 序

研究生教育肩负着国家高层次人才培养和创新创造的重要使命，是国家发展、社会进步的重要基石。研究生英语课程对于持续提高研究生的人文素养和专业能力，培养学生的家国情怀和创新精神，引导学生坚定文化自信、学术自信，成为有理想、有国际学术视野的高层次、创新性人才，从而更好地服务于国家的发展战略，都具有不可替代的重要作用。

为贯彻落实教育部印发的《高等学校课程思政建设指导纲要》，彰显立德树人根本宗旨，培养研究生的学术英语能力和跨文化交流能力，深入推进新时代研究生培养国际化，我们秉持以学生学习为中心的教育学理念，结合我国研究生英语学习实际需求和教学现状，策划编写了本套“研究生学术英语实用教程”系列教材，由《研究生学术英语阅读：理工类》《研究生学术英语阅读：人文类》《研究生学术英语写作：理工类》《研究生学术英语写作：人文类》《研究生学术英语视听说》共五册教材构成。

本套教材的编写原则与思路如下：

一、以立德树人为总目标，秉承以学生发展为中心、以学生学习为中心的理念，两个中心相辅相成，互为支撑。以学生发展为中心体现在将思政教育有机融入教材设计中，内容选择与问题设计体现中国学术贡献、学术诚信、文化自信、科学素养等思政元素。以学生学习为中心体现在内容设计围绕真实的学术活动展开，满足学生用英语进行专业学习、开展国际学术交流的现实需要。

二、着眼于跨文化学术交际，体现国际化人才培养的定位。本套教材将学术交流置于跨文化语境之中，注重培养学生的国际视野和跨文化学术交际意识，提升跨文化沟通中所需的学术交流能力和思辨能力。一方面，各分册的选材都兼顾中外学者、中英文学术语篇，提供比较分析的机会。另一方面，各分册所选语料都蕴含具体的学术体裁知识，为学生习得跨文化学术交流所需的各种学术英语知识提供必要的支持。

三、本着“在用中学”的编写理念，着力于学生多元能力培养。新时代深化研究生培养改革，必须着力增强研究生实践能力、创新能力等多元能力的培养。本套教材强调能力培养至上而非知识传授至上。各分册采用“以项目为导向”的学术英语教学方法，注重实际学术活动的参与和体验，以输入驱动输出，将听、说、读、写、译五项语言技能有机融合，强调综合语言应用能力、合作学习、自主学习能力的培养，激励学生通过讨论及修改反例等练习形式提升批判性思辨能力。

四、体现学术共性与学科差异。基于大类学科（如理工类、人文类）的特点，设计各分册，每个分册选材真实地道，来源多样，内涵丰富。同一单元涵盖多门学科，体现大学科特色，以支撑高校主流学科国际化人才的培养。

五、体现信息技术支撑。为实现教材编写目标，培养学生的自主学习能力，本套教材在各分册中都设计了让学生利用互联网自主查找文献或相关资源的教学活动。另外，全套教材采用线上与线下相结合的方式提供课堂教学资源和拓展学习资源。

本着上述编写原则和思路，"研究生学术英语实用教程"系列教材形成以下鲜明特色：

- **育人性。**各分册每个单元都有课程思政的元素，全套教材强调学术诚信和科学素养，力求将育人寓于学术英语知识传授和多元能力培养之中。
- **实用性。**全套教材所选语料来源于真实学术活动，内容设计贴近学生实际阅读、写作、听说需求，为其英语学习提供全面、切实、有效的指导。
- **针对性。**全套教材面向国内非英语专业研究生，在整个编写过程中，以学生为中心，关注他们的实际需求，聚焦他们在学习过程中的重难点，力求合理把握教学内容的难度，为学生提供丰富的、可学可用的语料。
- **可操作性。**全套教材练习形式多样，采用结对练习、小组讨论等形式凸显互动性和合作性，强调获得感。各分册均由八个单元构成，可满足 16 个标准课堂学时的教学需要，服务课堂操作。

作为体现学术共性与学科差异的学术英语系列教材，本套教材可以满足不同院校、不同学科研究生英语教学的需要。我们诚挚欢迎广大英语教师和各位学生在使用本套教材的过程中，能以各种方式提供反馈意见和建议，以便我们不断完善，打造一套启智润心、增知强能的系列精品教材！

陈新仁、黄燕

2022 年 4 月

前　言

《研究生学术英语阅读：理工类》是“研究生学术英语实用教程”系列教材之一。在具体呈现整套教材立德树人的总体编写理念、思路与特色的基础上，本册教材旨在满足我国理工类研究生进行学术英语文本阅读与写作的现实需要。为此，本教材聚焦学术英语阅读，提供大量不同题材的学术文本阅读训练，着力提升学生获得学术知识与习得学术规范的能力，并在此基础上帮助学生切实提高学术写作和交谈讨论等技能。

本册特色

本教材充分展现英语学术文体尤其是理工类学术论文的结构特征，详细介绍此类学术文本的篇章结构特征和语言风格，旨在培养和训练理工类研究生对于学术英语文本的阅读理解能力和写作能力，以期提高学生学术表达的规范性，增强学生的学术素养和学术意识，从而为他们未来的学术研究打好语言基础。作为研究生的学术英语阅读教材，本教材具有独特的整体性、系统性和创新性，适合研究生以及高年级本科生进行较为系统的学术阅读技能学习和训练。

教材构成

本教材以学科为基础，学术论文节选自近期发表的、影响力较大的学科期刊论文，共设八个单元，涉及征文征稿、论文标题和摘要、论文前言、文献综述、理论呈现、研究方法、讨论分析、审稿人意见等。每个单元开头都有一个简短介绍，供师生了解本单元的主要教学目标和内容。单元主体由七个部分组成，第一部分是单元介绍，第二至第七部分构成一个有机的整体：第二部分是与本单元主题阅读相关的短语表达，即在学术论文的某一部分所涉及的常用学术短语；第三部分是与本单元主题相关的阅读技巧与思考，旨在培养学生的学术文本分析能力和思辨能力，学生可在问题引导下进行课前阅读，教师可将课堂检查、讲解、测试相结合；第四部分为学术阅读与口语练习，要求学生在阅读完学术论文后，进行理性思考，讨论和学术论文结构有关的问题，培养学生的学术口语表达能力；第五部分为学术阅读和写作，培养学生恰当地使用学术语言撰写学术论文的能力；第六部分为课后练习，主要帮助学生积累并掌握常用的学术短语，巩固其对学术论文结构的理解，培养和提高学生判断信息、分析信息和综述信息的能力；第七部分为团队项目，培养学生利用所学的阅读技能解决实际问题的能力。

教学建议

本教材共有八个单元，建议每四个课时完成一个单元。课前，可通过“单元简介”了解本单元的主要教学目标和内容，并让学生提前自主学习第一部分的“常见表达”，在问题引导下阅读第二部分的两篇短文，教师在课堂上进行检查、讲解、测试。第三、四、五部分为课堂操练，建议采取各种互动形式开展多样化课堂活动，帮助学生熟悉了解相关主题阅读的内容和特征；第六部分为课后练习；第七部分是供学生课外团队学习、练习的项目，可以要求学生团队完成后在下一次课上进行课堂展示。教师可根据课堂时间安排等具体情况灵活搭配处理各部分内容。

编写分工

本教材由刘长江、饶辉担任主编，负责规划、选材、统稿、审校等工作；王秀文担任副主编，协助统稿；李迟、曹华参与编写。各单元分工情况如下：曹华负责第一、第二、第七单元；李迟负责第三、第四单元；王秀文负责第五、第六、第八单元。总主编陈新仁教授和黄燕教授认真细致地审阅了全部材料和书稿，并对书稿的修改、润色提出了宝贵的意见。在此，对他们表示衷心的感谢。

由于编者水平有限、编写时间仓促，书中难免有疏漏和错误之处，敬请广大同仁和英语学习者不吝批评指正。

编者

2022 年 5 月

Contents

Unit 1

Calls for Papers and Conference Programs

Part I
Introducing the Unit

In academic conferences or special journal issues, researchers will be formally invited to share their views and research advances in the fields of their interest. This formal invitation comes in a Call for Papers format. The call mainly describes the theme of the conference or the special issue, paper submission requirements and the deadline.

In this unit, we are going to explore the format and content of Call for Papers by reading and studying some selected samples.

Part II
Reading for Expressions

Study the following Call for Papers template and learn about some important expressions.

- **Name of the conference**
- **Date of the conference**
- **Link to the conference website**
- **It is a pleasure to invite you** to [Conference Name]. The conference is organized by [Department & Organization] and will take place in [Location] on [Conference Dates].

  [Brief history of your organization/conference and why recipients should submit.]
- **The theme** of [Conference Name] will be [Conference Theme].
- **Topics of interest**

  [List of Topics]
- **Guide for authors**

  The deadline to submit abstracts is [Submission Deadline].

  To submit your abstract, please click on the following link: [Link to the abstract management system log in page or online conference form.]

  (Insert any relevant information, guidelines and links.)
- **Important dates**

  Deadline for submission:

  Notification of acceptance:

  Deadline for final paper submission:
- **Organizing committee**

  [Roles and Names of the Organizing Committee]

  For any enquiries regarding the programme, please contact: [Email Address]

  For all general enquiries, please contact: [Email Address]

  We look forward to seeing you at [Conference Name].

  Sincerely,

  [Name of the Chair]

(Retrieved from Ex Ordo website.)

Part III
Reading for Ideas

Passage A

Pre-reading tasks:

1. Make a list of some important aspects that a typical case of Instructions to Authors may cover.
2. What is the significance of reading the Instructions to Authors before you draft a research paper?

How to Use Instructions to Authors

In considering where to submit your paper, you might have looked at some journals' Instructions to Authors to learn more about the journals' scopes, audiences, or requirements. If you have not yet obtained the instructions for the journal you chose, do so before starting to write. Typically, these instructions appear on the website of the journal.

If you do not find Instructions to Authors immediately, keep looking. Sometimes their location on the journal website is not initially apparent. Also, Instructions to Authors can have a variety of other names, such as Information for Authors, Guide for Authors, and Submission Instructions. If, after careful searching, you still do not find the instructions, consider asking a more experienced researcher or a librarian for help or contacting the office of the journal.

Read the Instructions to Authors thoroughly before starting to prepare your paper. Among questions these instructions may answer are the following:

- Does the journal include more than one category of research article? If so, in what category would yours fit?
- What is the maximum length of articles? What is the maximum length of abstracts?

- Does the journal have a template for articles? If so, how can it be accessed?
- Does the journal post supplementary material online, if applicable? If so, how should this material be provided?
- What sections should the article include? What guidelines should be followed for each?
- What guidelines should be followed regarding writing style?
- How many figures and tables are allowed? What requirements does the journal have for figures and tables?
- In what format should references appear? Is there a maximum number of references?
- In what electronic format should the paper be prepared? Should figures and tables be inserted within the text, or should they appear at the end or be submitted as separate files? Is there an online submission system to use?

Underline, highlight, or otherwise note key points to remember. Then consult the Instructions to Authors as you prepare the paper. Following the instructions from the outset will save time overall.

Also look carefully at some recent issues of the journal. Pay particular attention to those aspects of editorial style that tend to vary widely from journal to journal. These aspects include the style of literature citation, the use of headings and subheadings, and the design of tables and figures.

Shortly before submitting your manuscript, check the Instructions to Authors again, and ensure they have been followed. If the instructions include a checklist, use it. By following the instructions carefully, you will facilitate publication of your manuscript from the time you begin to draft it.

(Adapted from *How to Write and Publish a Scientific Paper* by Gastel, B. & Day, R. A., Westport: Greenwood Press, 2016.)

Fill in the blanks:

Before you draft a research paper, it is of great importance for you to read the Instructions to Authors carefully. Failure to follow these instructions may cause the delay of the preparation, submission and publication of your manuscript. A typical Instructions to Authors usually contains the (1) ________ of the journal, the maximum (2) ________ of articles and abstracts, the (3) ________ for articles, the (4) ________ for writing style, the (5) ________ format, the (6) ________ format of the paper, and relevant submission information.

Passage B

Pre-reading tasks:

1. What important details should a Call for Papers contain?
2. What skills can you adopt when reading a Call for Papers?

The Content of a Call for Papers

In academic conferences or special journal issues, the organizers or editors will craft a Call for Papers in a clear and compelling way to ask people from an academic community to present their research. The researchers, on the other hand, read the Call for Papers in an effort to scan for important information about the conference or special issue and details for submission of papers. More often than not, they can read the following parts in the Call for Papers:

- Title, location and date of the main event, and deadline for submission of papers, including the time of day. This makes it possible for researchers to quickly evaluate whether they can make the commitment to the event and to the time involved in submitting the paper.
- Introductory text—referencing issues with an overview of the event or project—setting expectations for what they could apply to be part of.
- Description of types of papers sought—including content and format.
- A checklist of steps for submitting a paper, including a basic list of the elements that are needed, and including word counts per section. This should include the deadlines (again), the related links to more detailed information and online submission forms.
- Criteria for acceptance—beyond complying with the basics of the paper format, what elements would the best papers be expected to include. This acts as a guide or rubric for the paper writers.
- Relevant links to FAQs, past events and contact information in case someone has questions.

(Retrieved from wikiHow website.)

Fill in the blanks:

The researchers who might be interested in presenting their research would (1) _______ for key details in the Call for Papers. So the Call for Papers should make these key details clear and reader-friendly: (2) _______, (3) _______ and (4) _______ of the main event, and (5) _______ for submission of papers; list of topics; (6) _______ information.

Part IV Reading for Speaking

Read the Calls for Papers in the following two passages, and then discuss the questions in groups.

Passage A

Conference Announcement and Call for Papers of Nutrition and Nurture in Infancy and Childhood

Bio-cultural perspectives

Three-day international, interdisciplinary conference

Monday 12th, Tuesday 13th and Wednesday 14th June, 2017

Grange-over-Sands, Cumbria

Our eighth international, interdisciplinary conference is being organized by the Maternal and Infant Nutrition and Nurture Unit (MAINN), University of Central Lancashire.

The conference convenor is Fiona Dykes, Professor of Maternal and Infant Health (MAINN, UCLan).

The conference links closely with the international journal *Maternal & Child Nutrition* (Wiley-Blackwell Publishing) that has its editorial office in MAINN. Senior Editors are Victoria Hall Moran (MAINN, UCLan) and Rafael Perez-Escamilla (Yale University, USA).

There is a growing understanding of the complex interactions between sociocultural, biological, political and economic influences upon infant and child feeding, eating and nutrition. The conference aims to:

- illuminate sociocultural, political and economic influences upon infant and child feeding practices;
- explore the nature of relationships within families in connection with various types of nutritive and nurturing behavior in infancy and childhood;
- increase understandings of breastfeeding as a bio-psychosocial activity;
- enhance understanding of the complex interactions between sociocultural, psychological and biological factors in infant and child feeding, eating and nutrition;
- focus on key initiatives that may impact upon practices related to infant and child feeding, eating and nutrition.

Keynote Speakers

- Anna Axelin, Associate Professor, Department of Nursing Science, University of Turku, Finland;
- Nita Bhandari, Head of WHO Collaborating Centre for Research, Community Based Action and Programme Development in Child Health, Society for Applied Studies, India;
- Tanya Cassidy, Marie Skłodowska-Curie Fellow (EC funded), MAINN, UCLan, UK;
- Stephan Dombrowski, Health Psychologist, University of Stirling, UK;
- Suzanne Filteau, Professor of International Nutrition, London School of Hygiene and Tropical Medicine, UK;
- Rafael Perez-Escamilla, Professor of Epidemiology & Public Health, School of Public Health, Yale University, USA.

Participants

Participation and attendance are encouraged from practitioners, academics and students across a spectrum of disciplines to include:

- anthropologists and medical sociologists;
- biological scientists;
- dieticians and nutritionists;
- general practitioners;
- infant feeding specialists, peer supporters and lactation consultants;

- maternal and child health, pediatric and neonatal nurses;
- midwives and health visitors;
- pediatricians and neonatologists;
- public health specialists;
- psychologists.

Abstract Requirements (Deadline 12 Dec. 2016)

Papers or posters are invited on:

- Infant and child nutrition and feeding (to include biological, social, cultural, psychological, political, economic and practice issues). The scope includes fetal and neonatal nutrition, infant and child nutrition, feeding and eating, up to and including adolescence.
- Nurturing the infant–parent relationship. The scope includes infants, parents, staff and/or organizations.

Thirty-minute papers will be presented at concurrent sessions, and posters will be displayed and discussed during designated poster sessions. Abstracts should be submitted on the online submission form on the conference website: http://www.uclan.ac.uk/conference_events/nutrition-and-nurture-infacy-childhood.php.

All abstracts will be reviewed by the Conference Scientific Review Committee chaired by Professor Fiona Dykes. The abstract must include the following:

- title of abstract;
- author/presenter name(s), institution represented, postal address, email address;
- primary contact person for the conference information;
- corresponding author for liaison regarding publication of the abstract;
- an introduction, methods, results and conclusions.

You should also pay attention to the following issues:

- the abstract should not include subheadings;
- the abstract should be referenced, citing between 2 and 4 references;
- the references should be presented in Harvard APA.

Length should be no more than 700 words (including title, author information and references). Please state your preference for a paper or poster presentation. Please also supply a short biography of each author.

You can access the book of abstracts for the 2015 Conference from http://onlinelibrary.wiley.com/doi/10.1111/mcn.v11.S2/issuetoc.

Maternal & Child Nutrition journal would like to invite you to submit your abstract for publication in the MAINN published conference proceedings. The proceedings will have open online access. Please note that abstracts will be subject to peer review. Should your abstract be accepted for publication in this special issue of *Maternal & Child Nutrition*, it will not preclude you from subsequently publishing your research in full in any journal. Please indicate if for any reason you prefer not to have your abstract published in the book of proceedings.

Maternal & Child Nutrition

Impact Factor: 3.505

ISI Journal Citation Reports © Ranking 2015: 10/120 (Pediatrics); 21/78 (Nutrition & Dietetics)

MAINN website:

http://www.uclan.ac.uk/research/explore/groups/maternal_and_infant_nutrition_and_nurture_unit.php

The Grange Hotel

The conference venue is The Grange Hotel, Grange-over-Sands, which is situated on the fringe of the Lake District in beautiful surroundings. For details on the charms of this stylish location go to: http://www.grange-hotel.co.uk/.

Conference Booking and Enquiries

All presenters will be required to register for the conference and pay the fee which will be £395 for the three days, non-residential. However, if you cannot attend for the full three-day event, a daily rate is available at £135.

For conference enquiries please contact Liz Roberts, Conference and Events, University of Central Lancashire, Preston PR1 2HE.

Email: healthconferences@uclan.ac.uk

Tel: +44 (0)1772 893809

Conference website: www.uclan.ac.uk/conferences

For academic queries please contact Professor Fiona Dykes on fcdykes@uclan.ac.uk.

For queries regarding publishing your abstract in *Maternal & Child Nutrition* please contact Dr Victoria Hall Moran on mcnjournal@uclan.ac.uk.

(Retrieved from LinkedIn website.)

 Questions:

1. Can you generalize what important aspects the submission guidelines section contains in this Call for Papers?
2. Why are the keynote speakers especially introduced here?
3. Why does the Call for Papers point out that "All abstracts will be reviewed by the Conference Scientific Review Committee"?

Passage B

Call for Papers: Special Issue on "Energy-Water-Food Nexus"

March 2016

With continuous population increase and economic growth, challenges on securing sufficient energy, water, and food supplies to meet the demand are also amplifying. The close linkages of the three sectors give rise to the need for tackling the challenges with a nexus approach. Information shared and interpreted jointly between these three sectors is important for better understanding the complicity of the energy-water-food (E-W-F) nexus and taking integrated approaches for their management. Studies and discussions on the issues relating to concept, research framework, technology innovations, and policy implementation of the nexus are needed to facilitate this understanding. In addition, governance and climate change can guide the development of innovations and policies in the energy, water and food sectors; hence, are important aspects in the nexus analysis. This special issue will provide a platform for presenting the latest research results on the E-W-F nexus issues and identifying remaining gaps. We welcome theoretical, methodological and empirical research papers, best practice and implementation on the relevant issues in science, technology and policy. Review and opinion papers that provide critical overviews on the state of the art, research gaps and the further directions of the research are also welcome. In particular, the water and food issues related to future clean energy systems are most relevant to this special issue.

Topics of interest of this Special Issue include, but are not limited to the following aspects of the integrated energy systems:

- trends and tools in nexus;
- concept of nexus;
- nexus from the energy perspective;
- nexus from the water perspective related to energy;
- nexus from the food perspective related to energy;
- existing tools and models in analyzing the nexus;
- new approaches and models needed for the analysis;
- nexus framework and governance;
- research framework for the nexus analysis;
- land, climate and energy constraints on water and food sectors;
- governance challenges in the E-W-F nexus;
- governance in supporting innovations in renewable energies and mitigating climate change impacts;
- uncertainties in the E-W-F interactions and constraints on clean energy development and investment;
- investment and finance for energy and water infrastructure;
- future clean energy technologies and systems under water and food constraints;
- water needs in the energy systems such as power plants, fuel refineries, renewable energy development, and carbon capture & storage, etc.;
- energy needs for water supply and agriculture: extraction, transportation, and disposal of water, livestock production, fertilizer production, irrigation, food transportation, etc.;
- agriculture and land-use impacts on future energy systems;
- future urban energy systems with considerations of water and food security;
- implementation and best practices;

- technology innovations for supporting global secure access to clean energy and water;
- reductions in water and wastewater utility operational costs through energy efficiency improvements;
- case studies of innovative technologies and policies in municipalities and industries for energy and water savings;
- energy and water consumption and balance flows of urban and industrial systems.

This Special Issue solicits original work on integrated energy systems (more than one energy systems should be considered in the paper) that must not be under consideration for publication in other venues. Full papers are solicited for reviews. Authors should refer to the Applied Energy author guidelines at: http://www.journals.elsevier.com/applied-energy/ for information about content and formatting of submissions.

Submission Format and Guideline

All submitted papers must be clearly written in excellent English and contain only original work, which has not been published by or is currently under review for any other journal or conference. Papers must not exceed 30 pages (one-column, at least 11pt fonts) including figures, tables, and references. A detailed submission guideline is available as "Guide to Authors" at: http://www.journals.elsevier.com/applied-energy.

All manuscripts and any supplementary material should be submitted through Elsevier Editorial System (EES). The authors must select as "SI: Energy-Water-Food Nexus" when they reach the "Article Type" step in the submission process. The EES website is located at: http://ees.elsevier.com/apen/default.asp.

All papers will be peer-reviewed by at least two independent reviewers. Requests for additional information should be addressed to the guest editors.

Editors in Chief & Managing Editor

Prof. Jinyue Yan

Guest Editors

Prof. Junguo Liu

Professor, South University of Science and Technology of China, China

liujg@sustc.edu.cn

Prof. Arjen Y. Hoekstra

Professor, University of Twente, Enschede, The Netherlands

a.y.hoekstra@utwente.nl

Prof. Hao Wang

Professor, China Institute of Water Resources and Hydropower Research, China

wanghao@iwhr.com

Prof. Jianhua Wang

Professor, China Institute of Water Resources and Hydropower Research, China

wjh@iwhr.com

Prof. Chunmiao Zheng

Professor, South University of Science and Technology of China, China

zhengcm@sustc.edu.cn

Dr. Michelle T. H. van Vliet

Wageningen University, Wageningen, The Netherland

michelle.vanvliet@wur.nl

Dr. May Wu

Argonne National Laboratory, Argonne, USA

mwu@anl.gov

Prof. Benjamin Ruddell

Professor, Northern Arizona University, USA

Benjamin.Ruddell@nau.edu

Important Dates

Full paper submission: **November 30th, 2016**

Final decision notification: **June 1st, 2017**

Publication of special issue: **July 30th, 2017**

(Retrieved from ELSEVIER website.)

 Questions:

1. What is the basic format of the Call for Papers of a special journal issue?
2. Is it necessary for the editor to explain the key words "nexus approach" at the beginning of this Call for Papers?
3. Passage A is a Call for Papers of an academic conference while Passage B is a Call for Papers of a special journal issue. How do the two Calls for Papers differ in terms of format and content?

Part V Reading for Writing

A Call for Papers should introduce the theme of the conference or the special issue, paper submission requirement and deadline information. Read Passage A in "Reading for Speaking" and write a summary of no less than 200 words that answers the following questions:

- What is the purpose of a Call for Papers?
- What is the organization of a typical Call for Papers?
- What can be done to make sure that the Call for Papers is written in a catchy, informative and scannable manner?

Exercises

I. Translate the following sentences into English with the words or phrases in the brackets.

1) 2021年中国人工智能会议征文通知；本次会议的征文范围如下（包括但不限于该范围）。(Call for Papers; topics of interest)

2) 本次会议由中国科技发展战略研究院主办、《中国科技论坛》编辑部承办。(sponsor; undertake)

3) 会议的主题是：差异、分歧、对话。(theme)

4) 本次学术会议将邀请国内外著名专家、学者作主题报告。(keynote reports)

5) 欢迎各界专家、学者以及研究生代表踊跃投稿、参会。(contribute to)

6) 大会形式主要包括特邀报告、口头汇报和海报展示等。(invited lectures; oral presentations; poster presentations)

7) 论文应为未在学术会议或学术期刊公开发表过的原创论文。(original)

8) 请通过会议网站下载论文全文模板，并通过会议网站在线提交论文全文。(template; submit)

9) 会议论文将集结为论文集，并提交 Web of Science 和 Scopus 等数据库索引。(indexes)

10) 论文经评审后择优推荐至以下学术期刊发表。(recommend)

II. Read the following Call for Papers, and then do the exercises.

Call for Papers

Looking Forward: The long-term implications of COVID-19 for transport and the environment

May 2021

COVID-19 dramatically changed the landscape of transportation in 2020. Human mobility became a matter of primary importance, as a virus that spreads through close contact traversed the world through the fast-moving and extensive transport routes of the 21st century. As a response to the pandemic, nearly every human on the planet was forced to modify both their daily travel habits and long-distance travel plans. Long-distance travel, especially by air, has dropped precipitously due to both travel restrictions and fear of virus transmission in enclosed environments. Some people have acquired personal vehicles to avoid the use of shared modes of transport such as shared mobility and public transport while others have started to try shared bikes and E-scooters. Telecommuting has become routine for many around the world, and online shopping and home delivery have soared. Public transport ridership has plummeted in many cities around the globe. There is speculation that cities will decentralize in the future. Many of these changes have exacerbated existing social equity issues, and may reshape our economies in ways that are not yet fully understood.

Disruptions—especially when they extend for a period of months or years—may bring about lasting changes. Understanding how transportation systems suffered, adapted and recovered during COVID-19 can provide models for future crises. Whether and how COVID-19 has changed people's travel behaviors and preferences in the long-term is of paramount importance for future decisions on infrastructure development. How residential preferences evolve, and how transportation systems adapt to accommodate such changes are major problems that urban and transportation planners will face in the coming years. Whether COVID-19 will have a lasting impact on people's inclination to use public transport will also impact plans for transit-oriented and sustainable development. As countries begin to recover from the pandemic, it is critical that transportation planners and policymakers understand people's travel behaviors, preferences and choices that may be emerging and persisting in post-COVID times.

This Call for Papers invites ***contributions*** that illuminate how the COVID-19 pandemic has changed travel-related choices (e.g., daily travel, long-distance travel, tele-activities, and emerging transportation options) and, more importantly, to ***empirically elaborate on*** the long-term impacts on our transportation systems and the environment. We invite papers on the following topics:

- the long-term changes in tele-activities (e.g., telecommuting, online shopping, online schooling, telemedicine, and videoconferencing) and associated travel and environmental outcomes;

- the long-term effects of the COVID-19 pandemic on the ownership and/or use of different ground transportation systems, e.g., privately-owned vehicles, public transport, and shared mobility (e.g., carpooling, taxi, ride-sourcing, E-scooter and bike-sharing), as well as on non-motorized transport choices;
- the long-term effects of the COVID-19 pandemic on home and/or work location choices (the latter influenced by employers as well as by workers), and their implications for travel and environmental outcomes;
- the future of long-distance travel as influenced by COVID-19 and possible future pandemics;
- the adaptation of cities and public transport systems, the aviation industry (including airlines, airports and auxiliary service providers), and inter-city railway and coach services (e.g., planning, operation) to both the COVID-19 pandemic itself, and to changes in travel demand brought on by the pandemic;
- the differential impact of all the above on different populations and economic sectors, and the associated impact on transport equity.

Timeline:

Call for Papers issued: May 15, 2021

Submission deadline: February 28, 2022

Submission Method:

All ***submissions*** must be ***original*** and may not be ***under review*** by any other journals. All ***manuscripts*** will be ***submitted*** via the Transportation Research Part D online submission system. Author Guidelines: https://www.elsevier.com/journals/transportation-research-part-d-transport-and-environment/1361-9209/guide-for-authors.

Authors should indicate that the paper is submitted for consideration for publication in this special issue. When choosing manuscript "Article Type" during the submission procedure, click "COVID impacts", otherwise your submission will be handled as a regular manuscript.

All submitted papers should address significant issues ***pertinent to*** the themes of this issue and fall within the ***scope*** of Transportation Research Part D. ***Criteria for acceptance*** include ***originality***, contribution, and scientific merit. All manuscripts must be written in English with high scientific writing standards. Acceptance for publication will be based on referees' and editors' recommendations following a standard peer review process.

Submissions and inquiries should be directed to the attention of guest editors:

Dr. Pengyu Zhu

Division of Public Policy

Hong Kong University of Science and Technology

Email: pengyuzhu@ust.hk

Dr. Deborah Salon

School of Geographical Sciences and Urban Planning

Arizona State University

Email: dsalon@asu.edu

Dr. Abolfazl (Kouros) Mohammadian

Department of Civil, Materials, and Environmental Engineering

University of Illinois Chicago

Email: kouros@uic.edu

(Retrieved from ELSEVIER website.)

1. **Fill in the blanks with the italicized words or expressions from the text above. Change the form if necessary.**

    1) The professor was capable of writing things of startling ________.

    2) It is laid down that all candidates must ________ three copies of their dissertation.

    3) These issues were outside the ________ of the article.

    4) Our contracts are currently ________.

    5) Please keep your comments ________ the topic under discussion.

6) All ________ for the May issue must be received by Friday.

2. **Answer the following questions according to the text above.**

1) Why does the editor elaborate on the theme of the Call for Papers at the beginning part?

2) Can you outline the process of submitting a paper to the editors?

3) Is this Call for Papers user-friendly? Why or why not?

3. **Summarize the main points of the above Call for Papers with no more than 150 words.**

III. **The ideas in a Call for Papers can be well organized by using headings, subheadings and paragraphing skills. A clear-cut organization or format can help the readers understand the main ideas and find relevant information more effectively. Read the following Call for Papers, and then fill in the blanks with proper subheadings.**

Call for Papers

2018 IEEE International Conference on Image Processing

October 7–10, 2018 · Athens, Greece

The 25th IEEE International Conference on Image Processing (ICIP) will be held in the Megaron Athens International Conference Centre, Athens, Greece, on October 7–10, 2018. ICIP is the world's largest and most comprehensive technical conference focused on image and video processing and computer vision. The theme of ICIP 2018 will be "Imaging beyond imagination". The conference will feature world-class speakers, tutorials, exhibits, and a vision technology showcase.

(1) __________:

- filtering, transforms, multi-resolution processing;
- restoration, enhancement, super-resolution;
- computer vision algorithms and technologies;
- compression, transmission, storage, retrieval;
- multi-view, stereoscopic, and 3D processing;
- multi-temporal and spatio-temporal processing;
- biometrics, forensics, and content protection;

- biological and perceptual-based processing;
- medical image and video analysis;
- document and synthetic visual processing;
- color and multispectral processing;
- scanning, display, and printing;
- applications to various fields;
- computational imaging;
- video processing and analytics;
- visual quality assessment;
- deep learning for images and video;
- image and video analysis for the Web;
- image processing for VR systems;
- image processing for autonomous vehicles.

(2) __________

Authors are invited to submit papers of not more than four pages for technical content including figures and references, with one optional page containing only references. Submission instructions, templates for the required paper format, and information on "no show" policy are available at 2018.ieeeicip.org.

(3) __________

Authors of papers published in all IEEE Signal Processing Society fully owned journals as well as in *IEEE Transactions on Computational Imaging* and *IEEE Wireless Communication Letters* will be given the opportunity to present their work at ICIP 2018, subject to space availability and approval by the Technical Program Chairs of IEEE ICIP 2018.

(4) __________

Following the tradition that started in 2016, the ICIP 2018 Innovation Program Chairs will arrange an outstanding event with prominent speakers from the Industry.

(5) __________

Tutorials will be held on October 7, 2018. Tutorial proposals must include title, outline, contact information, biography and selected publications for the presenter(s), and a description of the tutorial and material to be distributed to participants. For detailed submission guidelines, please refer to the tutorial proposals page. Special Sessions and Challenge Session Proposals must include a topical title, rationale, session outline, contact information, and a list of invited papers/participants. For detailed submission guidelines, please refer the ICIP 2018 website at 2018.ieeeicip.org.

(6) ________

Special Session Proposals: November 15, 2017

Notification of Special Session Acceptance: December 15, 2017

Tutorial Proposals: December 15, 2017

Notification of Tutorial Acceptance: January 15, 2018

Paper Submission: February 7, 2018

Notification of Acceptance: April 30, 2018

Camera-Ready Papers: May 31, 2018

(Retrieved from IEEE ICIP 2018 website.)

Project

Work in groups. Collect 10 Calls for Papers of your interest after class. You need to:

1. Find out what information is necessary and what information is optional.
2. Find out the general structure of the Call for Papers.
3. Prepare a report about your findings and present it in class.

Checklist of a well-written Call for Papers		
Content	**Yes**	**No**
Titles, locations and dates of the main events		
General requirements		
Topics of interest		

(continued)

Checklist of a well-written Call for Papers		
Content	Yes	No
Submission format and guidelines		
Word limit		
Review process		
Editors' information		
Important dates		

Unit 2

Titles and Abstracts

Part I
Introducing the Unit

A title followed by an abstract gives readers the first impression of a research paper, which can help the readers to decide whether to read the full paper for its relevance to their own research. A title functions as a label, reflecting the content of the research paper with the fewest possible words. It should be written in a clear, complete and concise manner. Similarly, an abstract is a short but informative summary of the paper, describing the purpose, methods, results and conclusion of the research. It should contain the essence of the research paper.

In this unit, we will read and analyze the titles and abstracts of some journal articles to discover the structure and functions of the title and abstract of a research paper.

Part II
Reading for Expressions

Study the different forms of titles and the bold-faced expressions that are often used in the abstract section of a research paper.

Different Forms of Titles

A Noun/Gerund Phrase

- The Importance of Enterovirus Surveillance in a Post-Polio World
- Air Source Heat Pump In-Situ Performance
- Neutralizing Antibodies After COVID-19 Vaccination in UK Haemodialysis Patients
- Operationalizing the Net-Negative Carbon Economy

A Sentence

- Obesity Accelerates Hair Thinning by Stem Cell-Centric Converging Mechanisms
- Clusters of Flowstone Ages Are Not Supported by Statistical Evidence

Expressions in Abstracts

Introducing the Research Purpose

- **The objective was to examine** the effect of consuming breakfast on subsequent energy intake.
- **Our aim was to conduct a systematic review** through meta-analysis to assess the association of depression with the risk for developing diabetes.

Describing the Research Methods

- **Meta-analysis was applied to calculate** the combined effect values and their 95% confidence intervals.
- **To address this issue**, here we **developed** a conservation planning framework to prioritize highly protected MPAs in places **that would result in multiple benefits today and in the future**.
- Here we **assess the potential of** plant communities to keep pace with climate change through long-distance seed dispersal by migratory birds.

- Here we **estimate** probability distributions for these projections under the new scenarios using statistical emulation of the ice sheet and glacier models.

Giving Results/Conclusions of the Study

- We **found** that human-made radio waves have already swept over 75 of the closest stars on our list.
- **Our land-based result** broadly **supports a recent reconstruction** based on marine proxy data assimilation that suggested greater climate sensitivity than previous estimates.
- **Together, these data and models illuminate the fundamental differences and similarities between** neural codes for 3D and 2D space in the mammalian brain.
- **These data demonstrates that** the outer halo is not in dynamical equilibrium, as is often assumed.
- **These results open up the way** towards a fully integrated, scalable silicon-based quantum computer.
- These results are **a step** towards quantum error correction and quantum simulation using quantum dots.
- **Our flexible prioritization framework** could **help** to inform both national marine spatial plans and global targets for marine conservation, food security and climate action.
- **Our results challenge the popular claim that** people value partisanship over accuracy, and **provide evidence** for scalable attention-based interventions that social media platforms could easily implement to counter misinformation online.

Part III Reading for Ideas

Passage A

Pre-reading tasks:

1. What is the function of the title?

2. What is essential for a good title?

How to Create a Good Research Paper Title

In general, the title should reflect the aim and approach of the work. Depending on the audience (and the specificity of the journal), some of the background may have to be included. Rarely are results and conclusions even hinted at in the title. Let's look at each of these items through examples.

Unlike newspaper reports and marketing press releases, the title of a research or scientific paper should describe the aim of the research, not the results. Thus, a good title might be:

Impact of Temperature and Pressure on the Compositional Uniformity of Sputter-Deposited Aluminum Alloys

The following news-style title, on the other hand, is not appropriate:

Optimizing Temperature and Pressure Improves Sputter-Deposited Aluminum Alloy Films

Note that the good title is essentially a statement of the aim of the research. Often it is important to mention the approach used as well, though an experimental approach is generally assumed if it is not mentioned. If the study had been based on simulation (or some other approach), however, this would generally be included in the title:

Impact of Temperature and Pressure on the Simulated Compositional Uniformity of Sputter-Deposited Aluminum Alloys

The title should be as specific as possible while still describing the full range of the research. For example, if only one aluminum alloy was being studied, that specific alloy should be mentioned in the title. If only aluminum alloys are studied, the title shouldn't say "sputter-deposited metals" or "sputter-deposited alloys". On the other hand, the title shouldn't say "aluminum alloys" if gold was also included in the study. If the title had said "uniformity" rather than "compositional uniformity", the reader could easily have believed that the paper was about thickness uniformity or some other parameter. And if only sputter deposition was studied, then leaving this information out would make the title insufficiently specific.

A conflicting goal of the title is to be as short as possible (in 2011, JM^3 titles ranged from 4 to 21 words in length, with an average length of 11.5). Specificity can often be improved through the use of more words, but a title that is too lengthy may not be read. Finding the best compromise between descriptiveness and brevity is where the art of authorship comes into play. Going back to our example, here is a title that sacrifices too much specificity to obtain brevity:

Impact of Process Parameters on the Uniformity of Aluminum Alloys

A good test for your title is to answer these questions: Does the title of your manuscript, seen in isolation, give a full yet concise and specific indication of the research reported? Would someone interested in the exact topic of your paper, reading this title, be inclined to read the abstract?

Avoid being overly clever with the title—a pun or a play on words may be great fun, but it is unlikely to help your article be found by a search engine (and can be easily misunderstood by an international audience). Titles should also be free of jargon unlikely to be understood by those not intimately familiar with the topic, and should not contain acronyms or trade-marked terms. The overall goal should be a title that is clear and informative.

(Adapted from "How to write a good scientific paper: Title, abstract, and keywords" by Mack C. A. in *Journal of Micro/Nanolithography, NEMS, and MOEMS*, Vol. 11, 2012.)

Fill in the blanks:

The title of a research paper needs to state the (1) ________ and (2) ________ of the research, not the results. It should be (3) ________ yet informative, giving clues on the full (4) ________ of the research. A good title also strikes a balance between (5) ________ and (6) ________, describing the content of the research with the fewest words and attracting the targeted readers.

Passage B

Pre-reading tasks:

1. What is the purpose of the abstract in a research paper?
2. What are the main parts of an abstract?

How to Write an Abstract for a Research Paper

An abstract should be viewed as a miniature version of the research paper. The abstract should provide a brief summary of each of the main sections of the paper: introduction, materials and methods, results, and discussion. As Houghton (1975) put it, "An abstract can be defined as a summary of the information in a document." "A well-prepared abstract enables readers to identify the basic content of a document quickly and accurately, to determine its relevance to their interests, and thus to decide whether they need to read the document in its entirety" (American National Standards Institute, 1979b). The abstract should not exceed the length specified by the journal (commonly, 250 words), and it should be designed to define clearly what is dealt with in the paper. Typically, the abstract should be typed as a single paragraph. Some journals, however, run "structured" abstracts consisting of a few brief paragraphs, each preceded by a standardized subheading. Many people will read the abstract, either in the original journal or as retrieved by computer search. The abstract should (1) state the principal objectives and scope of the investigation, (2) describe the methods employed, (3) summarize the results, and (4) state the principal conclusions.

Most or all of the abstract should be written in the past tense because it refers to work done. The abstract should never give any information or conclusion that is not stated in the paper. Literature must not be cited in the abstract (except in rare instances, such as modification of a previously published method). Likewise, normally the abstract should not include or refer to tables and figures. (Some journals, however, allow or even require the abstract to include a graphic.)

(Adapted from *How to Write and Publish a Scientific Paper* by Gastel, B. & Day, R. A., Westport: Greenwood Press, 2016.)

Fill in the blanks:

An abstract is a short but informative (1) ________ of the research paper. It enables the readers to get the (2) ________ of the research paper quickly so they can decide whether the rest of the paper is worth reading. The main parts of an abstract include (3) ________, (4) ________ and (5) ________, (6) ________, and (7) ________.

Part IV
Reading for Speaking

Read the titles and abstracts in the following two passages, and then discuss the questions in groups.

Passage A

Efficacy and Safety of Integrated Traditional Chinese and Western Medicine for Corona Virus Disease 2019 (COVID-19): A Systematic Review and Meta-Analysis

Abstract

Corona virus disease (COVID-19) has now spread to all parts of the world and almost all countries are battling against it. This study aimed to assess the efficacy and safety of Integrated Traditional Chinese and Western Medicine (Hereinafter referred to as "Integrated Medicine") to COVID-19. We searched six major Chinese and English databases to identify randomized controlled trials (RCTs) and case-control studies (CCSs) of Integrated Medicine on COVID-19. Two reviewers independently screened, identified studies, and extracted data. Cochrane Risk of Bias tool and the Newcastle-Ottawa Scale were used to assess the quality of included RCTs and CCSs, respectively. Stata (version 13.0; StataCorp) was used to perform meta-analyses with the random-effects model. Risk ratio (RR) was used for dichotomous data while the weighted mean difference (WMD) was adopted for continuous variables as effect size, both of which were demonstrated in effect size and 95% confidence intervals (CI). A total of 11 studies were included. Four were RCTs and seven were CCSs. The sample size of including studies ranged from 42 to 200 (total 982). The traditional Chinese medicine included Chinese medicine compound drugs (QingFei TouXie FuZhengFang) and Chinese patent medicine (e.g., Shufeng Jiedu Capsule, Lianhua Qingwen granules). Compared with the control group, the overall response rate [RR = 1.230, 95%CI (1.113, 1.359), $P = 0.000$], cure rate [RR = 1.604, 95%CI (1.181, 2.177), $P = 0.002$], severity illness rate [RR = 0.350, 95%CI (0.154, 0.792), $P = 0.012$], and hospital stay [WMD = –1.991, 95%CI (–3.278, –0.703), $P = 0.002$] of the intervention group were better. In addition, Integrated Medicine can improve the disappearance rate of fever, cough, expectoration, fatigue, chest tightness, anorexia and reduce patients' fever, and fatigue time ($P < 0.05$). This review found that Integrated Medicine had better effects and did not increase adverse drug reactions for COVID-19. More high-quality RCTs are needed in the future.

(Adapted from "Efficacy and safety of Integrated Traditional Chinese and Western Medicine for corona virus disease 2019 (COVID-19): A systematic review and meta-analysis" by Liu M. et al. in *Pharmacol Res*, Vol. 158, 2020.)

Questions:

1. Does the abstract repeat most of the title words? Why or why not?
2. Does this abstract serve as a brief summary of the purpose, methods, results and conclusion of the research? If so, explain how.
3. Why does the author propose a specific direction for future research on Integrated Medicine?

Passage B

Warming Impairs Trophic Transfer Efficiency in a Long-Term Field Experiment

Abstract

In ecosystems, the efficiency of energy transfer from resources to consumers determines the biomass structure of food webs. As a general rule, about 10% of the energy produced in one trophic level makes it up to the next. A recent theory suggests that this energy transfer could be further constrained if rising temperatures increase metabolic growth costs, although experimental confirmation in whole ecosystems is lacking. Here we quantify nitrogen transfer efficiency—a proxy for overall energy transfer—in freshwater plankton in artificial ponds that have been exposed to seven years of experimental warming. We provide direct experimental evidence that, relative to ambient conditions, 4 °C of warming can decrease trophic transfer efficiency by up to 56%. In addition, the biomass of both phytoplankton and zooplankton was lower in the warmed ponds, which indicates major shifts in energy uptake, transformation and transfer. These findings reconcile observed warming-driven changes in individual-level growth costs and in carbon-use efficiency across diverse taxa with increases in the ratio of total respiration to gross primary production at the ecosystem level. Our results imply that an increasing proportion of the carbon fixed by photosynthesis will be lost to the atmosphere as the planet warms, impairing energy flux through food chains, which will have negative implications for larger consumers and for the functioning of entire ecosystems.

(Adapted from "Warming impairs trophic transfer efficiency in a long-term field experiment" by Barneche D. R. et al. in *Nature*, Vol. 592, 2021.)

Questions:

1. In what way does the title give a full, concise and specific introduction to the research?
2. How does the abstract highlight the core points presented in the title?
3. What strategies or skills can you think of when writing an abstract?

Part V
Reading for Writing

An abstract should contain the purpose, methods, results and conclusion of the research. Read Passage A and Passage B in "Reading for Speaking" and write a summary with no less than 200 words that answers the following questions:

- What does a good title usually involve?
- What are the integral parts of an effective abstract?
- Should the abstract echo the title in a research paper?

Exercises

I. **Read the following two abstracts. Compare the similarities and differences between them in terms of wording and structure.**

Abstract 1

锂–空气电池是一种具有高能量密度、环境友好等优点的最具潜力的下一代储能电池体系。然而，其正极电化学反应缓慢的动力学过程导致了锂–空气电池充/放电过电位高、能量效率低、倍率性能差，而且催化剂的不稳定性也导致电池循环寿命短。开发高效且稳定的正极催化剂材料是解决上述问题的主要途径，也是锂–空气电池未来研究的重点。本文总结近几年来锂–空气电池正极催化剂的研究进展，并结合本课题组研究工作，以催化剂种类为切入点，深入综述及讨论了锂–空气电池催化剂的发展和存在的问题，并且展望了未来锂–空气电池正极催化剂的设计思路及对催化剂表界面反应机理的研究，对未来开发出高效、实用化的锂–空气电池具有重要的意义。

（曹学成，杨瑞枝 . 锂–空气电池正极催化剂研究进展 . 科学通报 . 64: 32, 2019.）

Abstract 2

Solid-state lithium (Li)–air batteries are recognized as a next-generation solution for energy storage to address the safety and electrochemical stability issues that are encountered in liquid battery systems. However, conventional solid electrolytes are unsuitable for use in solid-state Li–air systems owing to their instability towards lithium metal and/or air, as well as the difficulty in constructing low-resistance interfaces. Here we present an integrated solid-state Li–air battery that contains an ultrathin, high-ion-conductive lithium-ion-exchanged zeolite X (LiX) membrane as the sole solid electrolyte. This electrolyte is integrated with cast lithium as the anode and carbon nanotubes as the cathode using an in situ assembly strategy. Owing to the intrinsic chemical stability of the zeolite, degeneration of the electrolyte from the effects of lithium or air is effectively suppressed. The battery has a capacity of 12,020 milliamp hours per gram of carbon nanotubes, and has a cycle life of 149 cycles at a current density of 500 milliamps per gram and at a capacity of 1,000 milliamp hours per gram. This cycle life is greater than those of batteries based on lithium aluminum germanium phosphate (12 cycles) and organic electrolytes (102 cycles) under the same conditions. The electrochemical performance, flexibility and stability of zeolite-based Li–air batteries confer practical applicability that could extend to other energy-storage systems, such as Li–ion, Na–air and Na–ion batteries.

(Adapted from "A highly stable and flexible zeolite electrolyte solid-state Li–air battery" by Chi X. W. et al. in *Nature*, Vol. 592, 2021.)

II. Read the following title and abstract, and then do the exercises.

Solar Storms May Trigger Sperm Whale Strandings: Explanation Approaches for Multiple Strandings in the North Sea in 2016

Abstract

The Earth's atmosphere and the Earth's magnetic field protects local life by shielding us against solar particle flows, just like the sun's magnetic field deflects cosmic particle radiation. Generally, magnetic fields can ***affect*** terrestrial life such as migrating animals. ***Thus***, terrestrial life is connected to astronomical interrelations between different magnetic fields, particle flows and radiation. Mass strandings of whales have often been documented, but their ***causes*** and underlying ***mechanisms remain unclear***. We ***investigated*** the possible reasons for this phenomenon ***based on*** a series of strandings of 29 male, mostly bachelor, sperm whales (Physeter macrocephalus) in the southern North Sea in early 2016. Whales' magnetic sense may ***play an important role in*** orientation and migration, and strandings may thus be triggered by geomagnetic storms. This ***approach is supported by*** the following: (1) disruptions of the Earth's magnetic field by solar storms can last about 1 day and lead to short-term magnetic latitude changes corresponding to shifts of up to 460 km; (2) many of these disruptions are of a similar magnitude to more permanent geomagnetic anomalies; (3) geomagnetic anomalies in the area north of the North Sea are 50–150 km in diameter; and (4) sperm whales swim about 100 km day, and may thus be unable to distinguish between these phenomena. Sperm whales spend their early, non-breeding years in lower latitudes, where magnetic disruptions by the sun are weak and thus lack experience of this phenomenon. "Naïve" whales may ***therefore*** become disoriented in the southern Norwegian Sea ***as a result of*** failing to adopt alternative navigation systems in time and becoming stranded in the shallow North Sea.

(Adapted from "Solar storms may trigger sperm whale strandings: Explanation approaches for multiple strandings in the North Sea in 2016" by Vanselow K. H. et al. in *International Journal of Astrobiology*, Vol. 17, 2018.)

1. **Fill in the blanks with the italicized words or phrases from the text above. Change the form if necessary.**

   1) There was no positive evidence that any birth defects had arisen _______ Vitamin A intake.

   2) The evidence does not _______ the argument.

   3) This test aims to _______ whether the virus is contagious.

   4) The advent of the automobile may have _______ the growth pattern of the city.

   5) He _______ his conclusions on the evidence given by the research.

   6) However, the best methods for improving health through diet _______.

2. **Answer the following questions according to the text above.**

   1) What are the linguistic features and discourse structures of the title and abstract?

   2) How is the coherence between the title and abstract achieved?

   3) After reading the title and abstract, are you inclined to read the rest of the paper? Why or why not?

3. **The following excerpt is taken from the conclusion part of this research paper. How does this part differ from its counterpart in the abstract?**

The astronomical-biological approach that solar storms may contribute to sperm whale strandings persists. Support for a causal relationship between cetacean strandings and geomagnetic storms ranges from long-term statistical correlations with solar activity, to documented coincidences for single events. In this context, the stranding of 29 sperm whales early in 2016 might have been triggered by the solar storms recorded on 20/21 December 2015 and 31 December 2015 / 1 January 2016, which also caused the auroras observed at the same time over northern Europe. The current findings thus offer a plausible explanation of the phenomenon of sperm whale strandings, especially in the North Sea and may also be of relevance to other animals migrating through comparable areas.

III. Read the following abridged research paper, and then do the exercise.

Three-Dimensional Printing of Graphene-Based Materials and the Application in Energy Storage

1. Introduction

Graphene, as a typical two-dimensional (2D) material, is constituted by a single layer of sp^2-bonded carbon atoms with a honeycomb crystal structure. Since the first discovery in 2004 by Novoselov and Geim, tremendous attention has been paid on graphene material, owing to the special sing-atom thick feature and bonding characteristics of carbon atoms, which bring in lots of unparalleled properties in mechanical, electrical, thermal, and optical fields, and so on. Because of these unprecedented properties, numerous application potential in areas such as biomedical, automotive, energy storage, and electronics has been forecasted for the 2D graphene material. Although 2D graphene nanosheets have presented great application potential in many fields, some inherent drawbacks restrict the realization and further expansion of the application potential, especially in energy-related areas. For example, the 2D graphene sheets tend to restack in the solution, leading to the reduction of the electron and mass transfer rate. Meanwhile, the 2D graphene sheets lack the porous structures which could offer charge, carries rapid transport channels. Three-dimensional (3D) graphene structure, with the properties of high electrical conductivity, improved structural stability, low density, high porosity, and large surface area, could largely eliminate the aforementioned issues. Therefore, the 3D graphene-based structures have received more attention on the application in energy-related topics. A lot of research efforts have been made on the preparation and the application realization of the 3D graphene-based structures.

Currently, different construction methods have been developed to fabricated 3D graphene. Based on the synthesis principles, they can be categorized into the template method, such as template-directed chemical vapor deposition and template-directed assembly synthesis, and the self-assembly method, such as the reduction method, cross-linking method, and sol-gel method. Although these methods are able to obtain 3D graphene structures with unique properties (ultra-low density, ultra-high porosity, high specific surface area, good electrical and mechanical strength), their shortcomings, such as exorbitant price, poor efficiency, and complicated procedure, limit the application in industry. To obtain the 3D graphene architecture with good properties, while with low price, high efficiency, and controllable procedures, the importation of new technology has been taken into consideration. With the development of advanced manufacturing field, many researchers are trying to apply the 3D printing technology into the construction of 3D graphene structures.

3D printing, also termed as additive manufacturing, is the "process of joining materials to make objects from 3D model data, usually layer upon layer, as opposed to subtractive manufacturing methodologies". Emerging as a group of bottom-up methods, 3D printing is revolutionizing the way of creating products. Increasing attention has been attracted from the academic and industry sides. As for 3D printing, several advantages over the conventional methods could be summarized. First, it enables the building of a large number of prototypes or functional components with complex geometries; those are not easy to design using traditional ways such as extrusion and molding. Second, the 3D printing techniques can create functional parts without the need for assembly and also shorten the design-manufacturing cycle. Thus, the production cost is largely reduced, which could increase the competitiveness. In addition, the AM technologies can broaden the applications of manufacturing due to the improvements of processes and advancements of modeling and design. AM also has the environmental advantages such as reducing waste, minimal use of harmful chemicals and usage of recyclable materials. Consequently, AM has numerous potential applications in various fields; e.g., electronics, sensors, microfluidics, aerospace, automotive, medical, energy storage, and so on. The ideas of integrating 3D printing with hybrid graphene materials is especially alluring because not only do they solve the problems of poor mechanical properties and inferior stability of the 3D graphene structures; however, they also reduce the difficulties in preparing large-sized structures by other synthesizing methods. Meanwhile, this integration could offer a promising approach to alleviate some of the technologies' limitations; such as broadening of the material selection of AM processes and the capability of constructing the nanodevice with complex geometry. However, there are still some difficulties and challenges; such as the limited 3D printing technologies being developed, the aggregation of nanomaterials in the solvent, and the unfavorable impact from the additives existing in the construction of 3D graphene-based structures by 3D printing.

For the past several years, a lot of research studies have been focused on better integrating 3D printing technology with hybrid graphene materials to construct functional 3D structures for different application scenarios, especially in the energy storage field. Fig. 1 schematically illustrated the combination of 3D printing process with graphene-based materials and the promising applications. The aim of this paper is to provide the readers the current status about the combination of 3D printing with hybrid graphene materials, focusing on the applications in energy storage. The review is structured as follows: Section 2 will focus on the different 3D printing technologies, mainly including direct ink writing (DIW), fused deposition modeling (FDM), inkjet printing, stereolithography (SLA), and on the construction of 3D graphene structures. Section 3 will focus on the application of some energy storage devices. Section 4 will discuss the current challenges and future research prospects.

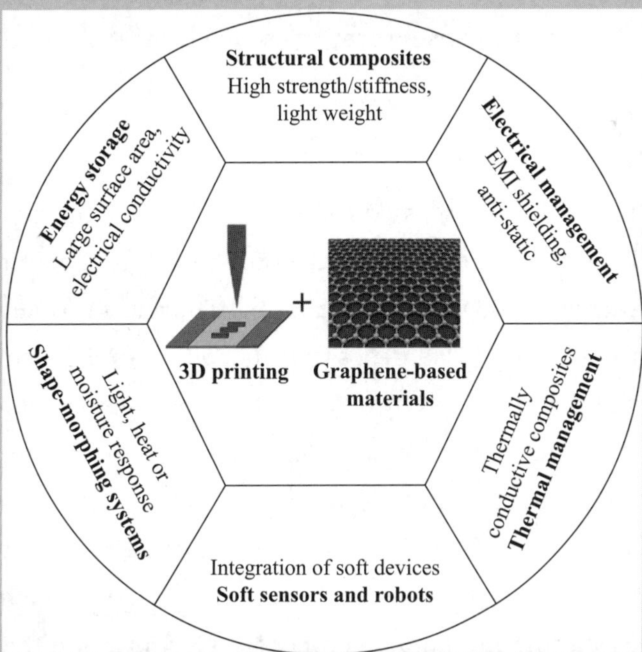

Fig. 1 Schematic for the combination of 3D printing process with graphene-based materials and the applications in different fields.

2. 3D printing methods for graphene-based materials

According to ASTM International, 3D printing can be classified into seven categories: (1) material extrusion (e.g., direct writing, fused deposition modeling), (2) powder bed fusion (e.g., selective laser melting, direct metal laser sintering), (3) directed energy deposition (e.g., laser net shape engineering), (4) material jetting (e.g., inkjet printing), (5) sheet lamination (e.g., laminated object manufacturing), (6) binder jetting, (7) vat photopolymerization (e.g., stereolithography). Among them, various methods have been applied to fabricate the 3D graphene structures. This section reviewed the most commonly used 3D printing technologies for graphene materials manufacturing.

3. Application of 3D-printed graphene-based material in energy storage

Graphene-based materials have received much attention in the energy storage application because of the outstanding electrical conductivity, large mechanical strength, specific surface area, and high chemical stability. Three-dimensional graphene architectures could further avoid the disadvantages of aggregation and overlaying of graphene materials. The 3D graphene synthesized by 3D printing methods could achieve higher mass loading and other tailored properties, which greatly facilitate the applications in energy storage devices such as supercapacitors and batteries.

4. Conclusions and prospects

In this review, we have discussed the recent advances on the adoption of 3D printing methods on the manufacturing 3D graphene-based architectures and the applications in energy storage areas. Four main 3D printing techniques, i.e., inkjet printing, direct ink writing, fused deposition modeling, and stereolithography are sequentially reviewed. In addition, two types of energy storage-related applications, supercapacitors and energy storage batteries, are summarized. From this review, it can be derived that significant progress has been made in 3D printing of graphene-based materials in the last few years because of the combined multiple advantages of 3D printing process and graphene materials, which could generate 3D complex structures with fascinating mechanical properties, electrical and thermal properties, thus enabling great potential in the applications of energy storage devices. However, some challenges still exist among the material preparation, printing technologies and device design.

For 3D printing methods being used to manufacture graphene-based materials, the key challenges include three aspects. (1) How to maintain the intrinsic properties of 2D graphene materials, including outstanding mechanical strength, electrical conductivity and large surface area. Although graphene materials have numerous excellent properties, the existing problems such as restacking, sub-graphitization, and defects generated during the synthesis process could largely influence the applications in energy storage. GO materials are more frequently applied in the 3D printing because of the availability, while the inferior electrical conductivity induced by the functional groups and defects is a major problem. Moreover, high-throughput, low-cost, and scalable preparation methods of high-quality graphene-based materials are still needed. (2) How to develop the printable inks or filaments based on graphene or GO materials with controllable viscosity and dispersity. The rheological characteristics of graphene-based composites are the most significant factors to determine the printability of the materials. Other behaviors, such as substrate-compatibility and drying behavior, are also important. To address these factors, binders, solvents, and additives are generally used. However, the ideal inks should contain as little non-capacitive ingredients as possible. The development of environmentally friendly, non-toxic graphene-based printing materials are also a big challenge. Other types of 2D materials, such as Mxenes and transition metal dichalcogenide, could also offer new prospects for the applications in 3D-printed energy storage devices. (3) How to develop new 3D-printing methods for preparing large scale 3D graphene-based structures with controllable spatial morphologies, resolution, and microstructures. The current, most often applied 3D printing techniques have their individual shortages; e.g., DIW usually needs a complex post-treatment for solvent evaporation, SLA is limited by the optical requirements of the materials, FDM has the main issue of poor accuracy and bad surface quality, and inkjet printing is usually restricted by the often-applied toxic ingredient. Common problems, such as nozzle-clogging, widely exist. Hence, developing new 2D and 3D printing processes, such as screen printing and roll-to-roll printing, are needed to prepare 3D graphene-based structures with high performance.

For the application of 3D-printed graphene-based material in energy storage, the challenges around the materials and 3D printing techniques as noted earlier still exist. The output performance of the printed electrodes is usually inferior to the conventional electrodes due to the low loading of graphene materials for the ink. Other important issues also challenge the development of this area. For instance, the current applications on energy storage focus on the electrode materials. The fully printed supercapacitors and batteries, which rely on the printing of both electrodes and electrolytes, as well as the integration of electrodes and electrolytes, would present better performance with higher manufacturing efficiency. Therefore, the future research should pay more attention to the manufacturing of electrolytes. The current complex post-treatments should also be simplified to meet the requirements of industry. Besides, the printed structures usually possess the features of porosity and anisotropy, which greatly degrade the mechanical performance of the energy storage devices. Thus, more efforts should be spent on balancing the mechanical performance and electrochemical properties. Meanwhile, the current printing experiment is conducted with a trial-and-error process, which is time consuming and not applicable in industry. To resolve this issue, feedback systems should be integrated into the printing process, which means the 3D printer could respond to the real-time change of the printing process. In addition, the current energy storage-related applications for 3D-printed graphene are focusing on supercapacitors and batteries. Other types of applications, such as fuel cells, solar cells, and electronic circuits, should receive more attention. The developing of all-component 3D-printed devices based on graphene materials would be another research direction.

In conclusion, the combination of 3D printing technologies with graphene-based materials are extremely promising, while the applications in energy storage devices are just at the beginning. After resolving the challenges, a large impact on energy storage areas could be expected in the future.

(Adapted from "Three-dimensional printing of graphene-based materials and the application in energy storage" by Wu, X. et al. in *Materials Today Advances*, Vol. 11, 2021.)

The following disordered sentences are taken from the abstract of the above paper. Rearrange these sentences into a well-organized abstract by numbering them from 1 to 7.

_______ The current progresses of energy storage applications, focusing on supercapacitors and energy storage batteries, were reviewed in detail.

_______ In this paper, we reviewed the recent research advances of 3D printing of graphene-based materials and discussed the applications in energy storage areas.

_______ Graphene-based materials have been extensively investigated in the energy-related applications owing to their unique properties, such as high conductivity and mechanical flexibility.

_______ Moreover, the future research challenges and prospects were provided in the last part, aiming at stimulating more significant research and industrial applications in this subject.

_______ The main 3D printing techniques applied in constructing graphene-based structures were summarized, and the characteristics of each method were briefly introduced.

_______ Three-dimensional (3D) graphene architectures could further strengthen their performance and facilitate the applications in energy storage.

_______ To fabricate 3D graphene architectures, the rapidly developed 3D printing technology presents a lot of advantages and has received much research attention.

Project

Work in groups. Collect the titles and abstracts of 10 research papers of your interest after class. You need to:

1. Identify the most frequently used words in the titles and abstracts.

2. Identify the most frequently used sentence patterns in the titles and abstracts.

3. Figure out the major types of content in the abstracts.

4. Prepare a PPT presentation of your findings to be reported in class.

Checklist of a well-written abstract		
Content	**Yes**	**No**
Introduction		
Materials and methods		
Results		
Discussion		

Unit 3

Introductions

Part I
Introducing the Unit

The introduction of a research paper serves the purpose of leading the reader from a general subject area to a particular field of research. It establishes the context of the research being conducted by summarizing current understanding of and background information about the topic, stating the purpose of the work in the form of a hypothesis, question, or research problem, briefly explaining the rationale, methodological approach, highlighting the potential outcomes your study can reveal, and describing the structure of the paper.

In this unit, we will learn to answer the following questions and list them as a rough outline:

- What is the current situation in a certain field?
- What are the problems?
- What is the significance of studying the subject?
- How do you solve the problems?
- How does this paper go further?

Part II
Reading for Expressions

Study the bold-faced expressions that are often used in the introductory section of a paper.

Introducing the Research Status

- Acoustic Emission (AE) signals **have been successfully used** for many years to monitor tool condition for conventional tools.
- The manufacturing business fraternity **has witnessed** dramatic changes in recent years.
- The development of advanced ceramic coatings **has received much attention** in the last few decades.
- **Recent studies suggest** that spermatid chromosome fragmentation and selective elimination of uniparental chromosomes after fertilization might be the possible cause of maize haploid formation.

Evaluating the Existing Studies

- Maize (*Zea mays* ssp. *mays*), as the world's highest grain production crop, **plays a particularly important role in** securing food, feed stock, and energy supply for an ever-increasing world population.
- Both methods **were found to be acceptable**.
- **The main difference in** machining between CFRP and metal **is** the chip formation mechanisms.
- **However, they should be carefully modified by** considering the operational conditions.
- **However, to the best of our knowledge, no** investigational new drug (IND) application **has been registered for** infectious diseases.
- **However, there are a large number of challenges to be overcome** before genome editing can be applied to patients.
- **The concept** of off-target genome editing **should be redefined** by the rapid growth of knowledge and experience on analysis of off-target genes and their effects.
- Current treatments for HSV-1 **do not eliminate** the virus from the site of infection or latent reservoirs in the trigeminal ganglia.

Describing the Research Methods

- In this paper, **new procedures are proposed to** detect tool breakage and to estimate tool condition (wear) by using AE.
- **We investigated** three possible mechanisms **to explain** the puzzles.

Introducing the Research Purpose

- **The objective of this paper is to develop** effective coating—economical alternative to diamond—for carbide drills for CFRP.
- **The objective of the present work is** dynamic task allocation through negotiation and preparation of local schedules for execution of customer order in a multiagent based holonic manufacturing system.
- **This approach**, we termed Haploid-Inducer Mediated Genome Editing (IMGE), **should greatly accelerate** future maize breeding via rapid generation of genome-edited pure DH lines with desired trait improvement in any elite background.

Stating the Research Significance

- **It offers high degree of** flexibility to deal with high level of uncertainties and unpredictable situations.
- **This establishes the need for** a control system and methodology that would allow the system entities to reconfigure, manifest agility.
- A new class of medicines **will be generated from** a series of consequences after clinical application of genome editing.

Part III Reading for Ideas

Passage A

Pre-reading tasks:

1. What do the authors mainly talk about in this excerpt?
2. What are the structural features of a good introduction?

The Purpose and Structure of the Introduction Section

The introduction serves the purpose of leading the reader from a general subject area to a particular field of research. It establishes the context of the research being conducted by summarizing current understanding and background information about the topic, stating the purpose of the work in the form of the hypothesis, question, or research problem, briefly explaining an author's rationale, methodological approach, highlighting the potential outcomes a study can reveal, and describing the remaining structure of the paper.

(Adapted from *Key Elements of the Research Proposal* by Curriculum Design and Writing Team, 2010.)

The importance of a good introduction:

Think of the introduction as a mental road map that must answer for the reader these four questions:

- What was I studying?
- Why was this topic important to investigate?
- What did we know about this topic before I did this study?
- How will this study advance our knowledge?

A well-written introduction is important because, quite simply, you never get a second chance to make a good first impression. The opening paragraph of a paper usually provides readers with their initial impressions about the logic of a author's argument, writing style, the overall quality of the research, and, ultimately, the validity of his findings and conclusions. A vague, disorganized, or error-filled introduction will create a negative impression, whereas, a concise, engaging, and well-written introduction will start readers off thinking highly of the analytical skills, the writing style, and the research approach.

(Retrieved from The Writing Center · University of North Carolina at Chapel Hill website.)

The introduction is the broad beginning of the paper that answers three important questions for the reader:

- What is this?

- Why am I reading it?
- What do you want me to think about / consider doing / react to?

A good author will organize the structure of the introduction as an inverted triangle of information. Organize the information so as to present the more general aspects of the topic early in the introduction, then narrow toward the more specific topical information that provides context, finally arriving at his/her statement of purpose and rationale and, whenever possible, the potential outcomes a study can reveal.

These are general phases used by a good author associated with writing an introduction:

Establish an area to research by:

- highlighting the importance of the topic, and/or
- making general statements about the topic, and/or
- presenting an overview on current research on the subject.

Identify a research niche by:

- opposing an existing assumption, and/or
- revealing a gap in existing research, and/or
- formulating a research question or problem, and/or
- continuing a disciplinary tradition.

Place his/her research within the research niche by:

- stating the intent and methods of the study,
- outlining the key characteristics of the study,
- describing important results, and
- giving a brief overview of the structure of the paper.

Mastering the structure of an introduction can help readers greatly improve their reading efficiency.

(Adapted from *Introductions and Conclusions* by Freedman et al., 2016.)

Fill in the blanks with the words given below:

Introduction is an important part of the scientific paper, mainly to answer the question "why research". And it is the first part of a paper to introduce the (1) _______ of the research and (2) _______ readers to understand the central content of the paper, so its main (3) _______ is to reflect the scientific nature and (4) _______ of the paper.

The content of the introduction generally includes three parts: The first part is (5) _______ of research comparison, (6) _______, development status, etc., which also includes a(n) (7) _______ review in a certain field. The second part puts forward the (8) _______ problems or problems that need to be solved so as to draw out the (9) _______ and significance of the author's own research. The third part explains the specific purpose and (10) _______ of the research.

According to the needs of different topics, the end of the introduction can introduce the components of the paper.

A. motivation	B. content	C. guide	D. unsolved	E. composed
F. innovation	G. function	H. literature	I. purpose	J. significance

Passage B

Pre-reading tasks:

1. What do the authors mainly talk about in this excerpt?
2. What are the basic principles that a good introduction must follow?

How to Develop a Good Introduction

Delimitations of the Study

Delimitations refer to those characteristics that limit the scope and define the conceptual boundaries of your study. This is determined by the conscious exclusionary and inclusionary decisions you make about how to investigate the research problem. Obviously, the first limiting step was the choice of research problem itself. However, implicit are other, related problems that could have been chosen but were rejected. These should be noted in the conclusion of your introduction.

Examples of delimitating choices would be:

- the key aims and objectives of your study,
- the research questions that you address,
- the variables of interest [i.e., the various factors and features of the phenomenon being studied],
- the method(s) of investigation, and
- any relevant alternative theoretical frameworks that could have been adopted.

Review each of these decisions. You need to not only clearly establish what you intend to accomplish, but to also include a declaration of what the study does not intend to cover. In the latter case, your exclusionary decisions should be based upon criteria stated as, "not interesting", "not directly relevant", "too problematic because...", "not feasible", and the like. Make this reasoning explicit!

The Narrative Flow

Issues to keep in mind that will help the narrative flow in your introduction:

Your introduction should clearly identify the subject area of interest. A simple strategy to follow is to use key words from your title in the first few sentences of the introduction. This will help focus the introduction on the topic at the appropriate level and ensures that you get to the primary subject matter quickly without losing focus, or discussing information that is too general.

Establish context by providing a brief and balanced review of the pertinent published literature that is available on the subject. The key is to summarize for the reader what is known about the specific research problem before you did your analysis. This part of your introduction should not represent a comprehensive literature review but consists of a general review of the important, foundational research literature (with citations) that lays a foundation for understanding key elements of the research problem.

Clearly state the hypothesis that you investigated. When you are first learning to write in this format it is okay, and actually preferable, to use a past statement like, "The purpose of this study was to..." or "We investigated three possible mechanisms to explain the...".

Why did you choose this kind of research study or design? Provide a clear statement of the rationale for your approach to the problem studied. This will usually follow your statement of purpose in the last paragraph of the introduction.

Engaging the Reader

The overarching goal of your introduction is to make your readers want to read your paper. The introduction should grab your reader's attention. Strategies for doing this can be to:

- open with a compelling story,
- include a strong quotation or a vivid, perhaps unexpected anecdote,
- pose a provocative or thought-provoking question,
- describe a puzzling scenario or incongruity, or
- cite a stirring example or case study that illustrates why the research problem is important.

NOTE: Only choose one strategy for engaging your readers; avoid giving an impression that your paper is more flash than substance.

The opening paragraph of your paper will provide your readers with their initial impressions about the logic of your argument, your writing style, the overall quality of your research, and, ultimately, the validity of your findings and conclusions. A vague, disorganized, or error-filled introduction will create a negative impression, whereas, a concise, engaging, and well-written introduction will start your readers off thinking highly of your analytical skills, your writing style, and your research approach.

Guidelines for a good introduction are as follows:

- The introduction should present first, with all possible clarity, the nature and scope of the problem investigated. For example, it should indicate why the overall subject area of the research is important.
- It should briefly review the pertinent literature to orient the reader. It also should identify the gap in the literature that the current research was intended to address.
- It should then make clear the objective of the research. In some disciplines or journals, it is customary to state here the hypotheses or research questions

that the study addressed. In others, the objective may be signaled by wording such as "in order to determine".

- It should state the method of the investigation. If deemed necessary, the reasons for the choice of a particular method should be briefly stated.
- Finally, in some disciplines and journals, the standard practice is to end the introduction by stating the principal results of the investigation and the principal conclusions suggested by the results.

The first four guidelines for a good introduction need little discussion, being reasonably well accepted by most scientist-writers, even beginning ones. It is important to keep in mind, however, that the purpose of the introduction is to introduce the paper. Thus, the first rule (definition of the problem) is the cardinal one. If the problem is not stated in a reasonable, understandable way, readers will have no interest in your solution. Even if the reader labors through your paper, which is unlikely if you haven't presented the problem in a meaningful way, he or she will be unimpressed with the brilliance of your solution. In a sense, a scientific paper is like other types of journalism. In the introduction, you should have a "hook" to gain the reader's attention. Why did you choose that subject, and why is it important? The second, third, and fourth guidelines relate to the first. The literature review, specification of objective(s), and identification of method should be presented in such a way that the reader will understand what the problem was and how you tried to resolve it.

To expand on that last point: Many authors, especially beginning authors, make the mistake of holding back their more important findings until late in the paper. In extreme cases, authors have sometimes omitted important findings from the abstract, presumably in the hope of building suspense while proceeding to a well-concealed, dramatic climax. However, this is a silly gambit that, among knowledgeable scientists, goes over like a double negative at a grammarians' picnic. Basically, the problem with the surprise ending is that the readers become bored and stop reading long before they get to the punch line. "Reading a scientific article isn't the same as reading a detective story. We want to know from the start that the butler did it."

In short, the introduction provides a road map from problem to solution. This map is so important that a bit of redundancy with the abstract is often desirable.

(Adapted from *How to Write and Publish a Scientific Paper* by Gastel, B. & Day, R. A., Westport: Greenwood Press, 2016.)

Fill in the blanks with the words given below:

When reading the introduction, we must focus on and analyze some basic features of the introduction as follows:

Get straight to the point and don't beat around the bush. Avoid (1) _______ descriptions of historical origins and research processes.

Be brief and comprehensive, (2) _______ the key points. When it is necessary to mention the research results and basic (3) _______ of others, only mark them in the form of references.

Review the history to have a focus, the content should be closely (4) _______ to the title of the article, around the title to introduce the (5) _______ with a few words.

Respect science and seek truth from (6) _______. In the introduction, evaluates the value of the paper appropriately, seeking truth from facts, words to science. Don't use inappropriate (7) _______ such as "innovative", "at first, this study first reported", "to fill the domestic blank", "has a(n) (8) _______ academic value", "the research content is reported for the first domestic" or "this study in the domestic and (9) _______ leading level".

The preface should not be divided into (10) _______, illustrations, lists, formula derivation and proof.

A. international	B. facts	C. sections	D. comments	E. high
F. highlighting	G. related	H. background	I. lengthy	J. principles

Part IV
Reading for Speaking

Read the introductions in the following two passages, and then discuss the questions in groups.

Passage A

Adaptive Compensation of Traction System Actuator Failures for High-Speed Trains

Introduction

High-speed trains with their fast and high loading capacities, have become more popular. In the recent years, a considerable number of studies have been focused on control design for the train systems. To achieve high speed and loading, the increasing of the automatic train operating control capabilities of high-speed train is required, which may increase the possibility of traction system failures. The traction system generating the traction/breaking force consists of rectifiers, inverters, PWMs (pulse width modulations), traction motors, and mechanical drives, etc., among which PWMs, traction motors, and mechanical drives are considered as actuators. Actuator failures are often uncertain in patterns, amplitudes, and time instances. These failed actuators may deteriorate the train performance severely, resulting in time delay or cancellation of the other trains. Therefore, it is crucial for the traction system of high-speed trains to study the effective failure compensation technologies.

During the past years, some results on fault diagnosis and fault-tolerant control for high-speed trains have been obtained, see, for example. It should be noted that the longitudinal dynamics of high-speed trains are usually used to study the automatic train control system or fault-tolerant control problem, since the control design is focused on the train handling, tracking and braking. Much of the existing work uses the longitudinal dynamic model with constants parameters, or the variable parameters with known upper bounds. However in practice, these parameters are time-varying and dependent on the track conditions. These constants or bounded variable parameters cannot represent the characteristics of the system dynamics well, which motivates the research to derive a new suitable model to describe the longitudinal dynamics of high-speed train for the control design. Specifically, a new piecewise constant model with unknown parameters is presented in this paper to solve the modeling problem.

On the other hand, when failures occur, it is necessary to utilize the failure compensation to guarantee the system stable and even asymptotic tracking. Until now, many results about the fault-tolerant control are available, see. It should be noted that in these results, the parameters of the plants are assumed either known or unknown but are modeled as unknown inputs with bounds. Adaptive techniques can be used to the control problem, in which the parameters are unknown, to achieve good tracking performance, which is suitable for high-speed trains. But, the unknown failure problem with the unknown piecewise constant parameters in the high-speed train has not been studied.

This paper is focused on the actuator failure compensation problem for the longitudinal dynamics of high-speed trains with traction system actuator failures. A piecewise constant model is used to describe the longitudinal dynamic system with its variable parameters. The design conditions, controller structure, and adaptive laws are derived for both healthy and faulty cases to construct the automated train control scheme.

The main contributions of this paper can be summarized as follows:

(1) For the variable high-speed train dynamics, a piecewise constant model is introduced to describe the longitudinal motion dynamics with traction system actuator failures.

(2) The adaptive controller with design conditions, structure and adaptive laws is developed for the healthy case when the piecewise constant parameters are unknown.

(3) For both the constant parameter model and piecewise constant parameter model, adaptive failure compensation schemes are designed for the high-speed train longitudinal motion system with unknown plant parameters and traction system actuator failures with unknown failure time and parameters.

The rest of this paper is organized as follows: In Section II, the dynamical model of high-speed trains are introduced, and the actuator failure compensation problem is formulated. In Section III, an adaptive control scheme is developed for the healthy system with unknown parameters, as the baseline adaptive system. A simulation study is presented to show the performance of the proposed method. In Sections IV and V, the failure compensation schemes for both constant parameter and piecewise constant parameter systems, are developed, respectively. Simulations for these two cases are also presented to verify the effectiveness of the failure compensation schemes. Finally, some conclusions are given in Section VI.

(Adapted from "Adaptive compensation of traction system actuator failures for high-speed trains" by Mao, Z. H., Tao, G., Jiang, B. & Yan, X. G. in *IEEE Transactions on Intelligent Tranportation Systems*, Vol. 18, No. 11, November 2017.)

Questions:

1. How is the introduction organized? How many parts can it be divided into?
2. What is the main difference between this study and previous studies?
3. What would you focus on if you were assigned to research on China's high-speed trains?

Passage B

The Development Trend of Artificial Intelligence in Medical: A Patentometric Analysis

Introduction

In recent ten years, Artificial Intelligence (AI) techniques have been booming globally, due to the accumulation of big data, innovation of algorithms, and improvement of the computer processing capacity. AI is already notably promoting the major progress of technology and industry, from autonomous vehicles to medical diagnosis to advanced manufacturing. In terms of the life and medical sciences field, AI techniques have broad applications, for instance, drug design, prediction of disease/drug risk, medical diagnosis, facilitating detection of cancer, medical image analysis, genomics, physiological parameter monitoring, and so on. These applications of AI techniques are expected to change the work pattern of doctors and complement traditional medical tools, availably enhancing the accuracy and efficiency of diagnosis.

The patent data is regarded as a unique resource for the study of technological change. Based on the patentometrics analysis, it can investigate the technique development trend. Meanwhile, the importance of the collaboration network in promoting knowledge production and diffusion has also been extensively studied, and collaborations can facilitate the improvement of research quality, resulting in more effective scientific production. Many studies are concerned on the co-author networks, co-citation networks, co-word networks, international collaborations, and cross-institution collaborations, in publications (e.g. papers and journals), which adopt the social network analysis (SNA) to study the relationships involved in the networks. However, to our knowledge, there is no bibliometric and collaboration network analysis based on patents in this inter-disciplinary research field.

Therefore, the patentometric is applied to gain a comprehensive view of the AI-medical techniques, and predict the development trend. The patent application year, technology life cycle, geographical distribution, and the collaboration relations of assignees are delved deeper into the status of technological development. SNA is carried out to investigate the collaboration network formed between institutions that are engaged in the AI-medical field.

(Retrieved from ELSEVIER website.)

Questions:

1. How is the introduction organized? How many parts can it be divided into?
2. In which part of the preface does the research topic of this study appear? Why?
3. How does the method like measurement proposed in this paper inspire your current research? Why?

Part V
Reading for Writing

An introduction plays a special role in the academic essay, and they frequently demand much of your attention as a writer. A good introduction, usually, follows a certain order of writing: The first is to introduce the nature and scope of the problem investigated. Secondly, briefly review the pertinent literature. Then, make clear the objective of the research and the method of the investigation. Finally, state the principal results of the investigation and the principal conclusions suggested by the results.

Please regroup the following sentences on micro-end-milling into a well-organized introduction according to the above requirements.

1) Acoustic Emission (AE) signals have been successfully used for many years to monitor tool condition for conventional tools.

2) However, the AE signal also includes extensive noise created by all the moving parts of the system.

3) Since the cutting force signals of the force transducers (or dynamometer) include very high noise created by the inertia forces of the machine oscillations, AE signals are a good alternative for tool condition monitoring.

4) In micro-machining very small amounts of metal are removed at extremely high rotational speeds. Cutting forces are very small at these metal removal rates, and extensive machine vibration is created by the high-speed spindle.

5) These techniques are good starting points to find similar methods for micro-machining applications.

6) In this paper, two new procedures are proposed to detect tool breakage and to estimate wear by monitoring tool condition in micro-machining applications.

7) However, they should be carefully modified by considering the operational conditions.

8) The developed tool condition monitoring procedures for micro-machining should be able to work with very small and noisy AE signals.

9) The following sections the theoretical background, proposed procedures, experimental set-up, and results are presented.

10) Proposed procedures use a single AE sensor, which can be easily attached between the work-piece, and the platform, which holds it.

11) The AE activity is monitored at a very small frequency range to minimize the noise and to have very high sensitivity by using specially designed sensors and hardware.

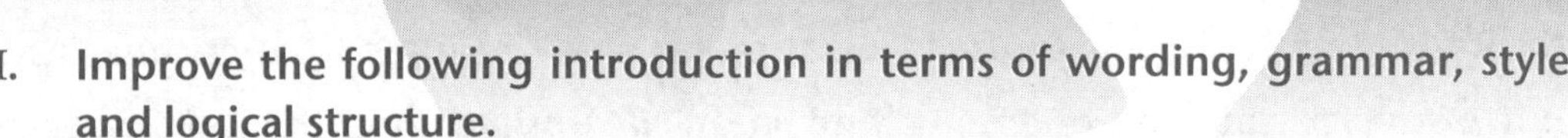

Exercises

I. **Improve the following introduction in terms of wording, grammar, style and logical structure.**

Six Cloned Calves Produced from Adult Fibroblast Cells after Long-term Culture

This study is conducted to test the cloning competence of skin fibroblast cells after prolonged in vitro culture, using an aged (17-year-old) elite bull. We know that animal cloning using cultured somatic cells offered us the possibility of targeted genetic manipulations like those that were performed in the mouse, those somatic cells remain competent for cloning after prolonged culture. Genetic manipulation of mouse embryonic stem cells changed mouse genetic research. However, embryonic stem cells are not available in other species. However, Live clones have been obtained from adult somatic cells in sheep, mice, and cows. Furthermore, some animals have been produced by cloning gene transfected fetal somatic donor cells.

Fortunately, to date, successful somatic cell cloning has been largely limited to the use of the donor cells either fresh or after short-term in vitro culture, which do not allow targeted gene manipulations.

In this paper, we reported that normal live clones were produced from cultured adult somatic cells in a cattle model after up to 3 months of culture. Our finding offers promise for producing site-specific genetically modified animals such as "gene knockout" animals by somatic cell cloning.

II. **Read the following excerpted introduction and then complete the exercises.**

The Role of Millimeter-Wave Technologies in 5G/6G Wireless Communications

Introduction

More than a century ago, in the 1890s, the capability of using electromagnetic waves to transmit signals wirelessly ***was demonstrated***, for the first time, in the famous wireless telegraphy experiment conducted by Nobel Laureate G. Marconi. It took around 80 years to turn it into commercial applications with which people can connect each other in real-time. ***Ever since then***, the technologies of mobile communications ***have evolved rapidly due to the developments in*** communication theory and multiplexing methods, microelectronics and ***integrated*** circuits (ICs), microwave circuits and antennas, and so on. ***Beginning from*** the 1980s, a new generation has ***emerged*** almost every decade. The first-generation (1G) of mobile communications ***was based on*** analog communications by using the frequency-division multiplexing access (FDMA). It ***only allowed*** voice signal transfer with limited and unstable spatial coverage. The second-generation (2G) ***uses*** digital communications where the time-division multiplexing access (TDMA) and code-division multiplexing access (CDMA) were ***adopted***. The 2G ***ensured*** a more stable link, a much wider coverage, and ***supported*** text messaging among users. The third-generation (3G) ***employed*** variations of advanced CDMA techniques and supported more versatile services, including, for the first time, multimedia data transfer. ***With the help of*** orthogonal frequency-division multiplexing (OFDM) and multiple-input multiple-output (MIMO) techniques, the fourth-generation (4G), including the 3.9G long term evolution (LTE) and 4G LTE-advanced ***was developed.*** They are able to ***offer*** a dramatically faster speed than 3G, ***providing*** a data rate of tens of megabytes per second. The revolutionary icon of the 4G era was the burgeoning ***widespread usage of*** smart-phones across the world, which changed the life style of human beings and the way people connect with each other. ***In terms of*** the frequency spectrums that are designated for the different generations of mobile communications, we can make two observations. ***First***, more frequency bands have been gradually released for a larger channel bandwidth that can meet the demands for higher data rates. ***Secondly***, all the released frequency bands are below 4 GHz, primarily ***due to*** two facts: 1) The electromagnetic waves below 4 GHz ***are less susceptible to*** blockage and weather changes and 2) the hardware chips and components are more cost-friendly and power-efficient.

With the fast growing of the number of consumer wireless devices in use and the expansion of the Internet of Things (IoT), the amount of mobile data transfer is almost doubled every year, surpassing that of the wired communications. The 4G mobile network infrastructure can ***no longer meet the needs*** for high-speed wireless data transmission. ***Therefore,*** from the second decade of the 21st century, the fifth-generation (5G) of mobile communications ***emerges*** with the ***outlook*** to the sixth-generation (6G). The 5G has been ***deployed*** in 2019 and is on the corner of massive commercialization. The International Telecommunication Union (ITU) has defined three major application scenarios for 5G New Radio (NR): They are the enhanced mobile broadband (eMBB), massive machine type communication (mMTC), and ultra-reliable low latency communication (URLLC). The 5G ***is expected to*** support a data rate of a few gigabits per second (Gb/s), a latency of milli-second, and a high volume of traffic density with greatly improved spectral, energy, and cost efficiencies. ***In order to meet these requirements***, a number of enabling network and hardware technologies have been developed, including ultra-dense networking, all-spectrum access, massive MIMO, and full-duplexing.

Importantly, from the frequency resource point-of-view, the uniqueness of 5G, ***in comparison with*** 3G and 4G, is the utilization of millimeter-wave (mmWave) frequencies in mobile communications, mainly due to two reasons. First, the sub-6 GHz spectrum has already been very crowded. Conceptual illustration of the 6G communication network that encompasses the 5G network. The mmWave 5G bands released by different countries. with distributed bands dedicated for cellular communications, satellite and aerial communications, and wireless local area networks (WLANs). ***On the contrary,*** at mmWave frequencies from 6 GHz up to 300 GHz, there are many unlicensed bands—the available spectrum is abundant. Secondly, the absolute bandwidth at mmWave frequencies is much larger than that at the lower microwave frequencies under the same relative bandwidth. The Third Generation Partnership Project (3GPP) has divided the 5G New Radio (NR) into FR1 band, i.e., 410–7125 MHz, and FR2 band, or also called mmWave band, i.e., 24.25–52.6 GHz. ***In addition to*** the narrow bands around 3.5 GHz and 4.9 GHz, many countries have released a number of mmWave bands for 5G NR communications in the *Ka*-band, *Q*-band, and even *E*-band. ***Consequently***, the system architecture, transceiver channels, ICs, passive and active components, and propagation channel modeling have become the main cutting edges of research.

Moving towards 2030 and beyond, ***due to*** the fast growth of new technologies such as virtual reality, vehicle-to-X network, unmanned aerial vehicle network, mid-earth-orbit (MEO) and low-earth-orbit (LEO) satellite network, and oceanic information network, the 5G communications would become insufficient. ***Therefore,*** very recently, several countries have called for or initiated research programs for the sixth generation (6G) of mobile communications. Although the specs of 6G, such as frequency bands, data rate requirements, have not been defined and finalized, its applications have been considered. A consensus for 6G has been reached—the 6G will be an intelligent mobile communication network of a much larger scale that encompasses the 5G. While the quasi-two-dimensional 5G network only covers a limited portion of lands on earth, the 6G network will ***extend into*** three dimensions and connects the satellites, aircraft, ships, and land-based infrastructures, providing a truly global coverage. The mmWave technologies will ***play an important role in*** enabling the various wireless links with enhanced speed and reliability superior to 5G. ***In addition***, the use of terahertz has also been proposed as a part of the frequency bands for 6G communications. ***However,*** the related key devices of terahertz chips, front-end components, and systems ***are not yet as mature and reliable as*** those operating at mmWave frequencies for long-distance communications with a high fidelity.

In this paper, the mmWave technologies that ***are important to*** 5G communications are reviewed, including the massive MIMO system architectures, beamforming chips, antennas for base stations (BSs) and user terminals (UTs), system measurement and calibration techniques, and wireless channel characterization. ***Then***, the challenges and requirements for future 6G communications ***are discussed***. The paper is organized as follows. Section II illustrates the system architectures of active multibeam arrays, ***including*** a comparison among different beamforming strategies. In Section III, the mmWave chips for beamforming are presented. The mmWave antennas for both BSs and UTs ***are described*** in Section IV, along with a discussion on several advanced antenna technologies. In Section V, the methods for system calibration and pattern measurement, RF testing, and system performance testing ***are reported***. Section VI presents a brief overview of channel characterization, followed by conclusions drawn in Section VII.

(Adapted from "The role of millimeter-wave technologies in 5G/6G wireless communications" by Hong, W. et al. in *IEEE Journal of Microwaves*, Vol. 1, No. 1, January 2021.)

1. **Fill in the blanks with the italicized words or expressions from the text above. Change the form if necessary.**

   1) The manufacturing business fraternity ________ dramatic changes in recent years.

   2) Different Document Type Definitions (DTDs) ________ for intended applications.

   3) Agility ________ remain unperturbed and provide reasonably good solution ________ disturbances and stands superior to its hierarchical counterpart.

   4) Multi Agent System (MAS) ________ the premise that a complex manufacturing system ________ a large number of small manageable agents.

   5) Specifically, a new piecewise constant model with unknown parameters is ________ in this paper to solve the modeling problem.

   6) ________ we found HELP was capable of modulating the HSV-1 reservoir in the TG.

   7) ________ to the best of our knowledge, no investigational new drug (IND) application has been registered for infectious diseases.

   8) ________, we examined if the intrastromal injection of HELP induces Cas9-specific IgG in the bloodstream.

2. **Most introductions have a relatively fixed logical structure sequence. Please analyze the introduction above and complete the table below.**

The Role of Millimeter-Wave Technologies in 5G/6G Wireless Communications

	Time	Name	Principle	Features
Background information	1890s		Electromagnetic waves to transmit signals wirelessly	
Literature review (development process)	1980s	1G	The frequency-division multiplexing access (FDMA)	Only allowed voice signal transfer with limited and unstable spatial coverage
		2G	The time-division multiplexing access (TDMA) and (1) ________	Ensured a more stable link, (2) ________, and supported text messaging among users

(continued)

<table>
<tr><th></th><th>Time</th><th>Name</th><th>Principle</th><th>Features</th></tr>
<tr><td rowspan="2">Literature review (development process)</td><td rowspan="2">1980s</td><td>3G</td><td>Variations of advanced CDMA techniques</td><td>Supported (3) ________, including multimedia data transfer</td></tr>
<tr><td>4G</td><td>(4) ________ and multiple-input multiple-output (MIMO) techniques</td><td>Offered a dramatically faster speed than 3G</td></tr>
<tr><td>Author's analysis</td><td colspan="4">First, more frequency bands have been gradually released for (5) ________.
Secondly, all the released frequency bands are below 4 GHz, primarily due to two facts:
1) The electromagnetic waves below 4 GHz are less susceptible to blockage and weather changes.
2) The hardware chips and components are (6) ________.</td></tr>
<tr><td>Evaluation</td><td colspan="4">The 4G mobile network infrastructure can no longer meet the needs for high-speed wireless data transmission.</td></tr>
<tr><td>Literature review (development process)</td><td>2019</td><td>5G</td><td>The enhanced mobile broadband (eMBB),
massive machine type communication (mMTC), and (7) ________</td><td>Is expected to support a data rate of a few gigabits per second (Gb/s), a latency of milli-second, and a high volume of traffic density with greatly improved (8) ________</td></tr>
<tr><td>Problems</td><td colspan="4">Moving towards 2030 and beyond, due to the fast growth of new technologies such as virtual reality, vehicle-to-X network, unmanned aerial vehicle network, mid-earth-orbit (MEO) and low-earth-orbit (LEO) satellite network, and oceanic information network, the 5G communications would become insufficient.</td></tr>
<tr><td>Research theme</td><td colspan="4">(9) ________, the system architecture, transceiver channels, ICs, passive and active components, and propagation channel modeling (10) ________ research.</td></tr>
<tr><td>Reasons of this study</td><td colspan="4">Therefore, very recently, several countries have called for or initiated research programs for (11) ________ of mobile communications.
The mmWave technologies will (12) ________ enabling the various wireless links with enhanced speed and reliability superior to 5G. (13) ________, the use of terahertz has also been proposed as a part of the frequency bands for 6G communications.</td></tr>
</table>

(continued)

	Time	Name	Principle	Features
Questions of this study	(14) ________, the related key devices of terahertz chips, front-end components, and systems (15) ________ those operating at mmWave frequencies for long-distance communications with a high fidelity.			
Layout of this article				

3. **Based on your understanding of this article and the table above, please write a summary of the introduction with no more than 300 words.**

III. To read a paper effectively, either as a learner or as a researcher, you must have a clear intention. First of all, you need to understand the topic of the article from the title and abstract. Second, you need to understand the structure which can be obtained from the introduction. Third, you need to understand the specific content and language style from the text. The following is an excerpt from a paper on flight control. The content that is not discussed in this unit has been truncated. Please analyze the text to understand the functions and structures of the introductory part in scientific writings.

Adaptive Model Inversion Flight Control for Tilt-Rotor Aircraft

Abstract

Neural-network augmented model inversion control is used to provide a civilian tilt-rotor aircraft with consistent response characteristics throughout its operating envelope, including conversion fight. The implemented response type is Attitude Command Attitude Hold in the longitudinal channel. Conventional methods require extensive gain scheduling with tilt-rotor nacelle angle and speed. A control architecture that can alleviate this requirement, and thus has the potential to reduce development time and cost, is developed. This architecture also facilitates the implementation of desired handling qualities and permits compensation for partial failures. One of the powerful aspects of the controller architecture is the accommodation of uncertainty in control as well as in the states. It includes an online, i.e., learning-while-controlling, neural network that is initialized with all weights equal to zero. Lyapunov analysis guarantees the boundedness of tracking errors and network parameters. Performance of the controller is demonstrated using a nonlinear generic tilt-rotor simulation code.

Introduction

① BOEING, Bell Helicopter Textron, Inc., and NASA are jointly working on a civilian tilt-rotor aircraft (CTR) that builds on the XV-15 and V-22 technologies and that they will extend to civilian applications. ② A CTR provides a unique challenge for fight-control augmentation because it displays a variety of handling characteristics as it converts from cruise fight to helicopter configuration. ③ This paper (1) ________ a powerful low-cost method to provide the CTR with consistent Level 1 responses throughout its operating envelope.

④ Feedback linearization is a (2) ________ used in nonlinear control applications, and there have been several advanced fight control demonstrations. Dynamic model inversion is the feedback linearization method employed in this study. This method is very (3) ________ in applications to high angle-of-attack fighter aircraft. The main drawback of dynamic model inversion is the need for high-fidelity nonlinear force and moment models that must be inverted in real time, which implies a detailed knowledge of the plan dynamics, and the approach tends to be computationally intensive.

⑤ (4) ________, dynamic model inversion is sensitive to modeling errors. The application of robust and/or adaptive control can alleviate this sensitivity and therefore the need for detailed knowledge of the nonlinearities. (5) ________, to date, the adaptive control literature has assumed linearity in control. This assumption is (6) ________ over the CTR operating envelope. The neural-network-based adaptive scheme applied here allows for nonlinearities and uncertainties in the controls as well as in the states.

⑥ Dynamic model inversion control is applied based on a single nominal operating point of the tilt-rotor aircraft operating in helicopter configuration, 30 kn, sea level at maximum gross weight. Operation at any other fight condition or configuration will result in an inversion error. Augmenting the model inversion with a linear on line neural network that is learning while controlling compensates for this error. The network update law is derived from a Lyapunov. Stability analyse is based on tracking error and network performance. This (7) ________ boundedness of both the tracking error as well as the network weights. In this work Euler angles were used to implement commanded acceleration response and attitude stabilization. A rate command application, (8) _______ timescale separation of translational and rotational dynamics, was used to provide trajectory control for an AH-64 helicopter in Ref. 10. Furthermore, we employ a network architecture that is linear in the weights, as in Refs. 9 and 10, but note that the guarantee of boundedness was extended to nonlinearly parameterized network structures in Ref. 11. A linearly parameterized network is simpler to implement and appears to be adequate for this application. The augmentation architectures presented here are applied to the XV-15 represented by the highdelity Generic Tilt-Rotor Simulator (GTRS) used at the NASA Ames Research Center. A comparison is made with the original stability and control augmentation system (SCAS) to (9) _______ the performance improvements in comparison with that obtained using conventional gain scheduling methods.

⑦ By design, a bandwidth separation between the tracking error dynamics and the command filter allows for easy implementation of the Aeronautical Design Standard-33D (ADS-33D) requirements for the different channels. The present work specifically addresses the implementation of Attitude Command Attitude Hold in the longitudinal channel. A similar architecture for Rate Command Attitude Hold augmentation and Turn Coordination in the lateral channels is presented in Ref. 16.

⑧ The first section contains a description of desired handling characteristics and associated terminology. The (10) _______ section outlines the implementation of the augmented-model inversion control architecture. The neural network structure used for this work is described next. Numerical results and evaluative remarks with respect to ADS-33D are included in the final section.

Flight-Control Augmentation for a Civilian Tilt-Rotor

Two common types of control augmentation for aircraft are (11) _______ as Rate Command Attitude Hold (RCAH) and Attitude Command Attitude Hold (ACAH). A good overview of various types of augmentation for the different control channels as used in the V22 are provided in Ref. 17. Reference 18 represents an example of the considerations involved in an approach procedure, including: 1) a schedule for the conversion of most angle with speed, from airplane to helicopter in the regular approach and vice versa for a missed approach procedure; 2) deployment or retraction of flaps depending on nacelle angle, speed, and glide slope; 3) switching between augmentation types; and 4) desired altitude and speed trajectories.

...

Neural-Network Augmented Model Inversion Architecture

This section details the architecture of the neural-network (NNW) augmented-model inversion as applied to the tilt-rotor aircraft, which is based on the applications as described in Refs. 9 and 10. Figure 2 contains a schema of the architecture used for implementation of ACAH control in the pitch channel. The (12) ________ architecture provided for excellent results in the longitudinal application. Preliminary results in the lateral channel shave shown similar performance.

...

NNW Structure and Adaptation

The NNW can consist of any linearly parameterized feed forward structure that (13) ________ approximately reconstructing the inversion error. For this demonstration a two-layer sigma-pi network was used.

...

Numerical Results

The XV-15 itself is (14) ________ by the comprehensive nonlinear GTRS code. This code includes complete augmentation, here referred to as original SCAS. This SCAS is gain scheduled with speed and with mast angle (though not with altitude). In the longitudinal channel, it provides ACAH and RCAH, depending on the mode selected by the pilot. The ACAH setting was used for the comparison in the following results.

...

Evaluation

ADS-33D states as one of the so-called Level 1 (most stringent) flying quality requirements: The pitch attitude shall return to 10% of the peak excursion, following a pulse input, in less than 10s (fight in Instrument Meteorological Conditions), and the attitude shall remain within the specified 10% for at least 30s.

...

(15) _______ the performance of the NNW adaptive control, a pilot model was developed. This model is able to perform such tasks as 1) follow desired altitude profiles; 2) follow desired speed profiles; 3) operate on both sides of the power curve; 4) convert, including flaps as well as nacelle angle changes; and 5) operate with different SCAS modes. The pilot model can provide lead, lag, or act as a PCI controller if necessary. Root locus methods were used to select desirable closed-loop characteristics. Reference 15 details the development of the longitudinal pilot model, which (16) _______ the mixing of control strategies mentioned earlier.

...

Conclusion

A tilt-rotor aircraft is a prominent candidate for augmentation of the longitudinal channel. The NNW augmented model inversion control is a valuable method for providing ACAH augmentation throughout the operational envelope of a tilt-rotor aircraft. The tracking errors and network parameters converge fast by design, and this provides for bandwidth separation with both the command filter as well as with actuator modes. The desired handling qualities can (17) _______ readily through the command filter. A relatively simple NNW (18) _______ provide stability for the operations considered. Similar strategies as applied to the pitch channel have been shown to provide good performance in the lateral channels. Because of the allowance of uncertainties and nonlinearities both in control (19) _______ in the state of the plant, a fixed-point (20) _______ is necessary, which is a mild assumption in the case of the tilt-rotor aircraft and with a proper design of the network. Further work will include an extension of the architecture, which should lead to fully automated trajectory following.

(Adapted from "Adaptive model inversion flight control for tilt-rotor aircraft" by Rysdyk, R. T. & Calise, A. J. in *Journal of Guidance, Control and Dynamics*. Vol. 22, No. 3, 1999.)

1. Read the introduction part and match the following functions with corresponding parts of the article.

1) Presenting an overview on current research on the subject. ( )

2) Giving a brief overview of the structure of the paper. ( )

3) Outlining the key characteristics of the study. ( )

4) Making general statements about the topic. ( )

5) Highlighting the importance of the topic. ( )

6) Formulating a research question or problem. ( )

7) Opposing an existing assumption. ( )

8) Stating the intent and methods of the study. ( )

2. Read the article and fill in the blanks with appropriate words or expressions in the table below. Change the form if necessary.

however	illustrate	follow	be capable of	as well as
combine with	represent	to further evaluate	ensure	be implemented
be sufficient to	effective	includes	in general	assumption
present	not valid	suggest	refer to	popular method

Project

Work in groups. You need to:

1. Collect the introductory section of 5 top journal articles and 5 MA theses written by Chinese students in English.
2. Evaluate the introduction of these 10 articles/theses according to the checklist below.
3. Compare them and find out how to improve the introduction of these theses.
4. Discuss with your group members and prepare a report for presentation in class.

Checklist of a well-written introduction				
Items		Yes	No	Not necessary
1	**Establish an area to research by:**			
	Highlighting the importance of the topic.			
	Making general statements about the topic.			
	Presenting an overview on current research on the subject.			
2	**Identify a research niche by:**			
	Opposing an existing assumption.			
	Revealing a gap in existing research.			
	Formulating a research question or problem.			
	Continuing a disciplinary tradition.			
3	**Place his/her research within the research niche by:**			
	Stating the intent and methods of the study.			
	Outlining the key characteristics of the study.			
	Describing important results.			
	Giving a brief overview of the structure of the paper.			
4	**Wording/Style**			
	Using correct tense.			
	Adopting academic expressions.			
	Utilizing well-structured/logical order.			
	Having too much detail.			
	Having sufficient details to introduce the study.			

Unit 4

Literature Reviews

Part I
Introducing the Unit

In science and engineering papers, generally, the literature review does not exist as a separate part. It is usually placed in the introduction/preface or becomes an article by itself. Undoubtedly, this part is very important in that a literature review surveys scholarly articles, books and other sources relevant to a particular issue, area of research, or theory, and by so doing, providing a description, summary, and critical evaluation of these works. Literature reviews are designed to provide an overview of sources you have explored while researching a particular topic and to demonstrate to your readers how your research fits into the larger field of study.

In this unit, we will read literature reviews from journal articles and conference papers to present the structure and content of a literature review as well as learn about its stylistic characteristics.

Part II
Reading for Expressions

Study the bold-faced expressions that are often used in the literature review of a paper.

Summarzing Results of Existing Research

- Holonic Manufacturing System (HMS) is **a subset of** Intelligent Manufacturing System (IMS).
- Herpes simplex virus type I (HSV-1) is **among the most common human viruses** with 50%–80% of the world population being seropositive.
- It **belongs to** the alpha subfamily of herpesviruses, which are enveloped viruses carrying double-stranded DNA, and **capable of** establishing latent infections in sensory neurons.
- The academic literature on AI in marketing may **be sorted into** four main types. **These are** (1) technical AI algorithms for solving specific marketing problems (**e.g., Chung et al., 2009; Chung et al., 2016; Dzyabura & Hauser, 2011, 2019**), (2) customers' psychological reactions to AI (**e.g., Luo et al., 2019; Mende et al., 2019**), (3) effects of AI on jobs and society (**e.g., Autor & Dorn, 2013; Frey & Osborne, 2017; Huang & Rust, 2018**), and (4) managerial and strategic issues related to AI (**e.g., Fountaine et al., 2019; Huang & Rust, 2020**).

Stating Contributions of Existing Research

- Acoustic Emission (AE) signals **have been successfully used for many years** to monitor tool conditional tools.
- The patent data **is regarded as** a unique resource for the study of technological change.
- **Based on** the patentometrics analysis, it can investigate the technique development trend.
- It **is achieved by bringing together** diverse AI literatures on algorithms (e.g., Bauer & Jannach, 2018; Davis & Marcus, 2015), psychology (e.g., Lee et al., 2018; Leung et al., 2018), societal effects (e.g., Autor & Dorn, 2013; Frey & Osborne, 2017), and managerial implications (e.g., Huang et al., 2019) to explore what those literatures can tell us about managing AI in marketing.

- **Importantly**, **previous** reports have **shown** that recombinant proteins compete for production in the mammary glands of transgenic animals.

Describing Defects of Existing Research Results

- This problem **becomes more complicated** in an open, distributed and dynamic platform.
- **Despite** the high prevalence, currently, **no** vaccine **is available for** HSV infection.
- **However**, the presence of foreign marker genes **interferes with** the expression of neighbouring endogenous genes and hampers phenotypic and genetic analyses.

Introducing Methods of Existing Research

- It **requires** new processing models with stronger decision-making and insight, **as well as** large-scale, high-growth and diversified process optimization capabilities.
- New manufacturing system approaches **are required** that provide manufacturers with the adaptability and responsiveness to compete in today's market.
- Here, we **established** a simple and safe method based on nucleofection and single-cell limited dilution to generate marker-free hLF BAC transgenic cows that produced a high level (4.5–13.6 g/L) of functional rhLF.

Part III Reading for Ideas

Passage A

Pre-reading tasks:

1. What do the authors mainly talk about in this excerpt?
2. How many types of literature reviews are presented here?

The Purpose and Types of Literature Reviews

The Purpose of a Literature Review is to:

- place each work in the context of its contribution to the understanding of the research problem being studied;
- describe the relationship of each work to the others under consideration;
- identify new ways to interpret, and shed light on any gaps in previous research;
- resolve conflicts amongst seemingly contradictory previous studies;
- identify areas of prior scholarship to prevent duplication of effort;
- point the way in fulfilling a need for additional research;
- locate your own research within the context of existing literature.

(Adapted from *The Literature Review: A Step-by-Step Guide for Students* (2nd ed.) by Ridley, D., Thousand Oaks: Sage Publishing, 2012.)

Types of Literature Reviews

It is important to think of knowledge in a given field as consisting of three layers. First, there are the primary studies that researchers conduct and publish. Second, the reviews of those studies that summarize and offer new interpretations are built from and often extending beyond the original studies. Third, there are the perceptions, conclusions, opinions, and interpretations that are shared informally that become part of the lore of field. In composing a literature review, it is important to note that it is often this third layer of knowledge that is cited as "true" even though it often has only a loose relationship to the primary studies and secondary literature reviews. Given this, while literature reviews are designed to provide an overview and synthesis of pertinent sources you have explored, there are a number of approaches you could adopt depending upon the type of analysis underpinning your study.

- **Argumentative Review**

This form examines literature selectively in order to support or refute an argument, deeply imbedded assumption, or philosophical problem already established in the literature. The purpose is to develop a body of literature that establishes a contrarian viewpoint. Given the value-laden nature of some social science research [e.g., educational reform, immigration control], argumentative approaches to analyzing the literature can be a legitimate and important form of discourse. However, note that they can also introduce problems of bias when they are used to make summary claims of the sort found in systematic reviews.

- **Integrative Review**

Considered a form of research that reviews, critiques, and synthesizes representative literature on a topic in an integrated way such that new frameworks and perspectives on the topic are generated. The body of literature includes all studies that address related or identical hypotheses. A well-done integrative review meets the same standards as primary research in regard to clarity, rigor, and replication.

- **Historical Review**

Few things rest in isolation from historical precedent. Historical reviews are focused on examining research throughout a period of time, often starting with the first time an issue, concept, theory, phenomena emerged in the literature, then tracing its evolution within the scholarship of a discipline. The purpose is to place research in a historical context to show familiarity with state-of-the-art developments and to identify the likely directions for future research.

- **Methodological Review**

A review does not always focus on what someone said [content], but how they said it [method of analysis]. This approach provides a framework of understanding at different levels (i.e. those of theory, substantive fields, research approaches and data collection and analysis techniques), enables researchers to draw on a wide variety of knowledge ranging from the conceptual level to practical documents for use in fieldwork in the areas of ontological and epistemological consideration, quantitative and qualitative integration, sampling, interviewing, data collection and data analysis, and helps highlight many ethical issues which we should be aware of and consider as we go through our study.

- **Systematic Review**

This form consists of an overview of existing evidence pertinent to a clearly formulated research question, which uses prespecified and standardized methods to identify and critically appraise relevant research, and to collect, report, and analyse data from the studies that are included in the review. Typically it focuses on a very specific empirical question, often posed in a cause-and-effect form, such as "To what extent does A contribute to B?".

- **Theoretical Review**

The purpose of this form is to concretely examine the corpus of theory that has accumulated in regard to an issue, concept, theory, phenomena. The theoretical literature review help establish what theories already exist, the relationships between them, to what degree the existing theories have been investigated, and to develop new hypotheses to be tested. Often this form is used to help establish a lack of appropriate theories or reveal that current theories are inadequate for explaining new or emerging research problems. The unit of analysis can focus on a theoretical concept or a whole theory or framework.

(Adapted from "Defining a literature" by Kennedy, M. M. in *Educational Researcher*. Vol. 36, No. 4, 2007.)

Fill in the blanks with the words given below:

Literature review should aim at a certain research topic and (1) _______ the current academic achievements. The purpose of the literature review is to (2) _______ the information that has been thought about and studied in the (3) _______ field of this research topic, and to systematically present, (4) _______ and comment on the efforts of the (5) _______ scholars on this topic. Before deciding on a research topic, there are usually several questions to consider: How much is known about the subject in the research field or in other fields; what studies have been completed; the success of previous suggestions and (6) _______; there are no new research directions and in short, literature review is the basis of all (7) _______ research. Usually, there are six types of literature reviews: (8) _______ review, integrative review, (9) _______ review, methodological review, systematic review and (10) _______ review.

A. summarize	B. theoretical	C. reasonable	D. specific	E. argumentative
F. historical	G. authoritative	H. integrate	I. explore	J. countermeasures

Passage B

Pre-reading tasks:

1. What do the authors mainly talk about in this excerpt?
2. What are the characteristics of a good literature review?

The Structure and Organizational Method of the Literature Review Section

Structure

Literature review usually consists of three parts: preface, main body and summary. The preface mainly explains the purpose of literature review, introduces the main concept, definition, scope of the review (scope of the issues involved), the date of the literature, the status of the issues and the focus of the debate.

The main part includes the main content of literature review. The literature can be reviewed in chronological order, as well as on different issues and viewpoints. In the review, the literature is integrated, analyzed and compared to clarify the research history, current situation and development direction of relevant issues, and find out the solved problems and unresolved problems. Emphasis is placed on the development trend of the current level of influence, so as not only to determine the direction of the research, but also to facilitate readers to understand the entry point of the research.

The conclusion part is to summarize the viewpoints in the literature. The reason lies in the correlation between the research problem and the previous related research. Readers can not only understand the past and present of the problem, but also look into the future, so as to propose the research problem or research hypothesis.

Ways to Organize Your Literature Review

- **Chronological of Events**

If your review follows the chronological method, you could write about the materials according to when they were published. This approach should only be followed if a clear path of research building on previous research can be identified and that these trends follow a clear chronological order of development. For example, a literature review that focuses on continuing research about the emergence of German economic power after the fall of the Soviet Union.

- **By Publication**

Order your sources by publication chronology, then, only if the order demonstrates a more important trend. For instance, you could order a review of literature on environmental studies of brown fields if the progression revealed, for example, a change in the soil collection practices of the researchers who wrote and/or conducted the studies.

- **Thematic ("Conceptual Categories")**

Thematic reviews of literature are organized around a topic or issue, rather than the progression of time. However, progression of time may still be an important factor in a thematic review. For example, a review of the Internet's impact on American presidential politics could focus on the development of online political satire. While the study focuses on one topic, the Internet's impact on American presidential politics, it will still be organized chronologically reflecting technological developments in media. The only difference here between a "chronological" and a "thematic" approach is what is emphasized the most: the role of the Internet in presidential politics. Note however that more authentic thematic reviews tend to break away from chronological order. A review organized in this manner would shift between time periods within each section according to the point made.

- **Methodological**

A methodological approach focuses on the methods utilized by the researcher. For the Internet in American presidential politics project, one methodological approach would be to look at cultural differences between the portrayal of American presidents on American, British, and French websites. Or the review might focus on the fund raising impact of the Internet on a particular political party. A methodological scope will influence either the types of documents in the review or the way in which these documents are discussed.

Other Sections of Your Literature Review

Once you've decided on the organizational method for your literature review, the sections you need to include in the paper should be easy to figure out because they arise from your organizational strategy. In other words, a chronological review would have subsections for each vital time period; a thematic review would have subtopics based upon factors that relate to the theme or issue. However, sometimes you may need to add additional sections that are necessary for your study, but do not fit in the organizational strategy of the body. What other sections you include in the body is up to you but include only what is necessary for the reader to locate your study within the larger scholarship framework.

(Adapted from *The Literature Review: A Step-by-Step Guide for Students* (2nd ed.) by Ridley, D., Thousand Oaks: Sage Publishing, 2012.)

Fill in the blanks with the words given below:

Literature review is a style that is different from research papers formed by researchers after they have read the literature on a certain topic (1) _______, through understanding, sorting out, (2) _______, comprehensive analysis and (3) _______. Retrieving and reading literature is an important (4) _______ for writing a review. The quality of a review depends largely on the author's knowledge of the latest literature (5) _______ to the topic. Without doing a good job of literature (6) _______ and reading, we will never write a good review. A good literature review can not only lay a solid theoretical foundation for the next (7) _______ writing and provide some (8) _______ opportunities, but also show the author's comprehensive ability to summarize, (9) _______ and comb the existing research literature, thus helping to improve the overall (10) _______ of the dissertation level.

A. evaluation	B. prerequisite	C. dissertation	D. in advance	E. analyze
F. summarizing	G. assessment	H. relevant	I. searching	J. extended

Part IV
Reading for Speaking

The literature review of the science, technology and medicine papers is included in the introduction or background section, or a separate review article. Analyze the literature review part in the introduction (background) section selected, and then discuss the questions in groups.

Passage A

Feedback-Feedforward Control Technique with a Comprehensive Mathematical Analysis for Single-Input Dual-Output Three-Level DC–DC Converter

Literature Review (from Introduction)

Nowadays, dc–dc converters are becoming increasingly interesting in providing high-quality energy to different electric loads, and recently, they are of major interfaces for delivering renewable energies to the consumers. Yet, due to the considerations such as number of components and cost issues, power electronic industries have been encouraged to design new generation of these circuits as multi-port dc–dc converters (MPCs). Accordingly, MPCs can provide simultaneous sources of energy with a compact assembly.

Until now, many topologies have been introduced for MPCs which are almost impractical for high voltage applications due to the high voltage stress across switches and diodes. In high voltage applications, the major challenge to MPCs is the voltage stress across semiconductor devices. High voltage stress on switches and diodes results in the higher costs, reduced efficiency, and increased size of passive components. Consequently, multilevel dc–dc converters (MLCs) are suggested as an effective solution to reduce the voltage stress on semiconductor devices, increase efficiency, and reduce the size of passive components. Among several reported topologies, single-input dual-output three-level dc–dc converter (SIDO-TLC) combines advantages of MPC and MLC, making it a promising topology for high voltage applications. In SIDO-TLC, the voltage stress across all power switches and diodes is reduced to only half of the boost output voltage, while simultaneously passive components size is shrunken and efficiency is increased. However, SIDO-TLC topology requires a complex control system to ensure fast dynamic, regulate the output voltages, and balance the series capacitors voltages at the boost output. In fact, SIDO-TLC is aimed at regulating two output voltages, and at the same time, the converter should assign a three-level control strategy. Consequently, there are multiple concurrent tasks for the converter, leading to complexity of the control system. As well, two proportional–integral (PI) controllers have been applied on SIDO-TLC that have their own related issues, such as the very slow dynamic and large undershoots/overshoots, degrading the stability of the system.

In this paper, a novel feedback-feedforward (FB–FF) technique is proposed to control SIDO-TLC. The proposed controller is designed by using small-signal dynamic model of the converter and phase-shifted pulse-width modulation (PWM) algorithm. The proposed controller consists of two main parts: (i) feedback (FB) control loops and (ii) feedforward (FF) control loops. To improve the transient responses of the dc–dc converter, two current controllers are assigned as adjunct blocks in the inner sections of the FB control loops. Also, a balancing FB loop is schemed for keeping the voltage differences of the boost output capacitors to zero. On the other hand, an external FF loop is assigned to decouple the introduced control inputs, resulting in an enhanced cross-regulation of the system. In this paper, the conventional PI controller by which SIDO-TLC has been implemented in the literature is considered as the benchmark to evaluate the merits of the proposed FF–FB controller. The evaluation of the proposed FB–FF controller is based on the dynamic responses of the system such as over-shoots, under-shoots, and settling time in addition to the steady-state performance such as load regulation.

Due to the significant advances in power electronics technology, there is a strong need for systems providing multiple dc outputs with different voltage levels. Subsequently, auxiliary circuits are commonly required in addition to the main power system, which they should be supplied at low voltages and powers. Accordingly, low-voltage low-power MLC is an attractive solution for applications such as portable devices, fuel cell systems, dc Nano-grids, bias supplies, personal computers, and so on. In this paper, SIDO-TLC implemented through the proposed control strategy is highly suitable for portable applications, in which high-speed low power electric drives are required. Moreover, the proposed control system can be executed through a fairly low switching frequency of 20 kHz, which can be readily implemented by a low-cost digital signal processor.

Furthermore, due to the low switching frequency and considering the fact that the voltage stress across all switches and diodes of the converter is only half of the boost output voltage, the efficiency will be substantially improved, making the converter highly suitable for portable devices. The novelty and contributions of the paper can be categorised as follows:

- A new control strategy is proposed for SIDO-TLC, through which the accuracy of the system is significantly improved compared to the previously implemented one.
- The proposed controller improves the dynamic response of SIDO-TLC. Accordingly, the voltage over-shoots and under-shoots at the outputs are reduced as well as decreasing the settling time of the system during load transients.
- The proposed controller also enhances the steady-state performance of SIDO-TLC. Consequently, the load regulations are improved at a wide range of loads.
- The suggested control technique is based on the straight forward FF and FB principles, implemented with a fairly low switching frequency of 20 kHz that can be readily run by a low-cost digital controller.
- The FB–FF controller implemented on SIDO-TLC is highly suitable for portable applications, where efficiency, cost, and speed are of great importance.

This paper is organised as follows. In Section 2, the operating principles of SIDO-TLC are explained. In Section 3, the dynamic small-signal model of SIDO-TLC and the proposed control technique are discussed. Section 4 carries out an assessment procedure for providing an offline adjustment of FB and FF coefficients. Then in Section 5, experimental and simulation results are provided. Finally, a conclusion is drawn in Section 6.

(Adapted from "Feedback-feedforward control technique with a comprehensive mathematical analysis for single-input dual-output three-level dc–dc converter" by Ganjavi, A. et al. in *IET Power Electronics*, Vol. 13, 2020.)

Questions:

1. What organizational method does the author use in the literature review part of the introduction?
2. What is the significance of literature retrieval and selection to your research?
3. How should we quote the results of previous studies? How can we achieve academic integrity when we do research and write papers?

Passage B

Development of a Haploid-Inducer Mediated Genome Editing System for Accelerating Maize Breeding

Maize (*Zea mays* ssp. *mays*), as the world's highest grain production crop, plays a particularly important role in securing food, feedstock, and energy supply for an ever-increasing world population. Over the past century, maize yield per unit land area increased over 7-fold due to the combined efforts of breeding and improvement in management (Mansfield & Mumm, 2014). The success of modern maize hybrids depends on breeding of elite parental inbred lines (Duvick, 2005). Traditional maize breeding based on genetic crosses requires 8–10 generations to introduce desirable alleles into a desired elite background and usually involves extensive background screening and large-sized populations to increase the chance of genetic recombination, which is very laborious, time consuming, and cost ineffective. Moreover, the results are usually unpredictable and not always accurate. Further, such an approach is often hindered by the linkage drag effect, when a desirable trait is closely linked to an undesirable trait, and separation of them either requires a prohibitory large-sized population or is nearly impossible due to the lack of recombination events in the particular region (Peng et al., 2014; Li et al., 2017a). Thus, there is an urgent need to develop a rapid and effective method for generating elite inbred lines combining multiple favorable traits for maize and other crops.

Doubled haploids (DH) technology, which is based on *in vivo* haploid induction, has become very popular for accelerating crop breeding, particularly in maize (Geiger, 2009). Nowadays, maternal haploids are routinely created by pollinating with a haploid inducer (HI) line such as Stock6 (Coe, 1959, with a haploid induction rate of 1%–2%) or other Stock6-derived inducers (such as CAU5, an inducer line developed by Professor Shaojiang Chen and his colleagues at China Agricultural University, with an induction rate up to 12%, Dong et al., 2014) in many maize breeding programs worldwide. Its chromosomes can be doubled spontaneously in nature at relatively lower frequencies or by artificial doubling by treatment with mitotic inhibitors such as colchicine, generating doubled haploid (DH) lines. Compared with traditional breeding, which could take up to eight generations to stabilize the genetic background of interest through repeated selfing or backcrossing, DH technology allows generation of pure homozygous lines within two generations (Ren et al., 2017). Recently, a gene responsible for haploid induction in maize, *MATRILINEAL (MATL)*, also known as *Patatin-Like Phospholipase A (ZmPLA1)* or *NOT LIKE DAD (NLD)*, which encodes a pollen-specific phospholipase, has been independently cloned by three groups (Gilles et al., 2017; Kelliher et al., 2017; Liu et al., 2017). Recent studies showed that knockout of the *MATL* homologous gene could also induce haploid formation in rice (Yao et al., 2018; Wang et al., 2019).

Since 2005, several toolboxes for genome editing, including zinc finger nucleases, transcription activator-like effector nucleases, and most recently the CRISPR (clustered regularly interspaced short palindromic repeat) system, have been developed and put into use in a number of plant species (such as *Arabidopsis*, rice, and wheat). In particular, the CRISPR/Cas9 system and its various improved versions recognizing different PAMs (protospacer-adjacent motifs) have been widely used to precisely modify important agronomic traits (yield, quality, biotic and abiotic stress resistance) in many crops, including maize (Chen, et al., 2019). However, a major technical hurdle of utilizing these technologies is the recalcitrant nature of most elite maize inbred lines for genetic transformation, and thus in most cases, maize lines with relatively high transformation efficiencies (such as HiII and B104) were often selected as the recipients for transformation and initial functional tests. Then, the selected transformation events with confirmed and desirable effects must be introgressed into elite commercial inbred lines via repeated backcrossing (at least six times to achieve 99.28% background purity), which is again laborious, time-consuming, and costly.

Recent studies suggest that spermatid chromosome fragmentation and selective elimination of uniparental chromosomes after fertilization might be the possible cause of maize haploid formation (Zhao et al., 2013; Li et al., 2017b). Intrigued by these findings, we wondered whether CRISPR/Cas9 could function to edit the genome during the process of HI-induced haploid formation when an HI line carrying a CRISPR/Cas9 cassette was used to pollinate a non-inducer maize line. If so, homozygous edited DH lines could be quickly generated by doubling the chromosome number of the edited haploid plants. We report here the successful generation of the genome-edited haploids for *ZmLG1* and *UB2* in the B73 background, using the CAU5 HI line carrying the CRISPR/Cas9 cassette for *ZmLG1* or *UB2*, respectively. This approach, we termed Haploid-Inducer Mediated Genome Editing (IMGE), should greatly accelerate future maize breeding via rapid generation of genome-edited pure DH lines with desired trait improvement in any elite background.

(Adapted from "Development of a haploid-inducer mediated genome editing system for accelerating maize breeding" by Wang, B. B. et al. in *Molecular Plant*, Vol. 12, 2019.)

 Questions:

1. Is the literature review written in a cohesive way? Explain your answer.
2. Have the reviewers interpreted and criticized the literature, or have they merely summarized it? Illustrate your answer with appropriate examples.
3. What kind of research do you expect the author to report in the main text of the paper?

Part V
Reading for Writing

Read the background below to learn the types of themes or ways to organize the review, and write a literature review on Traditional Chinese Medicine. The number of words should not be less than 400. Note the following three questions:

- What is the main purpose of the background?
- What is the theoretical perspective?
- What is the principal point, conclusion, thesis, contention, or question?

Rheum tanguticum Maxim. ex Balf belongs to the family Polygonaceae, and grows mainly in high-altitude areas in the southwest and northwest of China, such as Sichuan, Gansu, and Qinghai provinces. The rhizomes and roots of *R. tanguticum* (*Dahuang* in Chinese) are used in Chinese medicine for unloading the tapping product, clearing *re* (heat), purging *huo* (fire), removing pathogenic *huo* from the *xue* (blood), stimulating menstrual flow, and promoting diuresis and detoxification. The huge demand for *R. tanguticum* has caused excessive consumption in China. The reproductive rate of *R. tanguticum* is low and environment-dependent, and the wild resources of *R. tanguticum* are becoming endangered.

Genetic diversity involves organism complexity, ecosystem recovery, and species sensitivity to environmental changes. A lack of diversity reflected evidence for potential population endangerment. Various molecular markers were used to investigate the genetic diversity of *R. tanguticum*. Chen et al. discovered a relatively high genetic diversity at the species level and a low genetic diversity within populations of *R. tanguticum* by evaluating an SSR marker. These findings were in accordance with those of Wang et al. based on an ISSR marker. However, Hu et al. demonstrated a similar result at the species level, but an opposite result within and among populations of *R. tanguticum* using an ISSR marker. These studies of *R. tanguticum* genetic diversity involved limited materials, and their results were contradictory. Therefore, large samples and new molecular markers were required to reveal the real state of *R. tanguticum* genetic diversity.

The *mat* K gene (1500 bp) is a molecular marker for plant molecular systematics and evolution, and is located within the intron of the chloroplast gene *trn* K on the large single-copy section adjacent to the inverted repeat. Among various other molecular markers, the *mat* K gene sequence avoided any interference of heterozygosity and its evolutionary rate was relatively fast. Therefore, in recent years, the *mat* K gene has been employed as an important and powerful tool for examining intergenus and intragenus genetic diversity because of its high substitution rate.

This study aims to examine the genetic structure and genetic diversity of *R. tanguticum* within species, and the genetic differentiation within and among populations in China. The genetic diversity of *R. tanguticum* at the species level and within and among populations was investigated using the *mat* K gene sequences, and the population structure of *R. tanguticum* was clarified.

(Adapted from "Genetic diversity and population structure of *Rheum tanguticum (Dahuang)* in China" by Zhang, X. Q. et al. in *Chinese Medicine*, Vol. 9, No. 26, 2014.)

Exercises

I. **Selecting sources for a literature review: When selecting relevant sources to include in your literature review, you are advised to consider the following five elements of the material. Match the questions in the left column to the elements in the box by writing down the corresponding element in the right column. Note that each element may be used more than once.**

A. Provenance B. Methodology C. Objectivity

D. Persuasiveness E. Value

	Questions to be considered	Elements considered
1	What are the author's credentials? Is the author one of the major research authors in the field?	
2	Is the author's perspective even-handed or biased?	
3	Are contrary viewpoints considered or is certain pertinent information ignored to prove the author's point?	
4	Was the work published in a prestigious journal?	
5	Is the work one of the seminal works in the field?	
6	Does the work ultimately contribute in any significant way to the understanding of the subject?	
7	Are the methods and procedures used to identify, gather, and analyse the data appropriate to address the research problem? Is the sample size appropriate? Are the results effectively interpreted and reported?	
8	Are the author's arguments and conclusions convincing?	

II. **Structuring a literature review: Read the following literature review (bold type) in the introduction below. Analyse how this review is structured and explain why you come to this conclusion by completing the table.**

Introduction

Artificial intelligence (AI) in marketing is currently gaining importance, due to increasing computing power, lower computing costs, the availability of big data, and the advance of machine learning algorithms and models. We see wide applications of AI in various areas of marketing. For example, Amazon.com's Prime Air uses drones to automate shipping and delivery. Domino's pizza is experimenting with autonomous cars and delivery robots to deliver pizza to the customer's door. RedBalloon uses Albert's AI marketing platform to discover and reach new customers. Macy's On Call uses natural language processing to provide an in-store personal assistant to customers. Lexus uses IBM Watson to write its TV commercial scripts, "Driven by Intuition". Affectiva, based on affective analytics, recognizes consumers' emotions while they are watching commercials. **Replika, a machine learning-based chatbot, provides emotional comfort to consumers by mimicking their styles of communication. It has even been asserted that AI will change the future of marketing substantially (Davenport et al., 2020; Rust, 2020).** However, academic marketing research to date provides insufficient guidance about how best to leverage the benefits of AI for marketing impact.

The academic literature on AI in marketing may be sorted into four main types. **These are (1) technical AI algorithms for solving specific marketing problems (e.g., Chung et al., 2009; Chung et al., 2016; Dzyabura & Hauser, 2011, 2019), (2) customers' psychological reactions to AI (e.g., Luo et al., 2019; Mende et al., 2019), (3) effects of AI on jobs and society (e.g., Autor & Dorn, 2013; Frey & Osborne, 2017; Huang & Rust, 2018), and (4) managerial and strategic issues related to AI (e.g., Fountaine et al., 2019; Huang & Rust, 2020).**

The fourth literature stream, managerial issues related to AI, is currently dominated by consultants gravitating to the latest hot topic, and largely lacks a solid academic basis, albeit there are some recent studies trying to tackle strategic marketing issues. **Examples include unstructured data for various areas of marketing (Balducci & Marinova, 2018), analytics for consumer value in healthcare (Agarwal et al., 2020), machine learning prediction for mobile marketing personalization (Tong et al., 2020), in-store technology (e.g., robots, smart displays, or augmented reality) for convenience or social presence (Grewal et al., 2020), and AI for personalized customer engagement (Kumar et al., 2019).**

To facilitate the strategic use of AI in marketing, we develop a three-stage framework, from marketing research, to marketing strategy (segmentation, targeting, and positioning, STP), to marketing actions (4Ps/4Cs), for strategic marketing planning incorporating AI. This strategic AI framework is based on a more nuanced perspective of the technical development of AI, existing studies on AI and marketing, and current and future AI applications. It can be used for strategic marketing planning, for organizing the existing AI marketing studies, and for identifying research gaps in AI marketing.

This paper contributes to the strategic application of AI in marketing by developing a framework that guides the strategic planning of AI in marketing in a systematic and actionable manner. **It is achieved by bringing together diverse AI literatures on algorithms (e.g., Bauer & Jannach, 2018; Davis & Marcus, 2015), psychology (e.g., Lee et al., 2018; Leung et al., 2018), societal effects (e.g., Autor & Dorn, 2013; Frey & Osborne, 2017), and managerial implications (e.g., Huang et al., 2019)** to explore what those literatures can tell us about managing AI in marketing. Marketing is an applied field, and using the more foundational literatures to inform marketing practice is an important role for marketing academia. This paper also contributes to strategic marketing research by providing a systematic and rigorous approach to identifying research gaps that bridge strategic AI marketing practice and research.

(Adapted from "A strategic framework for artificial intelligence in marketing" by Huang, M. H. & Rust, R. T. in *Journal of the Academy of Marketing Science*, Vol. 49, 2021.)

Complete the following table according to your analysis.

Checklist of structuring approaches for literature reviews			
1	**Chronological approach**	yes	no
	Does the topic require some historical background?		
	Do your sources indicate a significant shift in thinking?		
2	**Thematic approach**	yes	no
	Can these sources be grouped based on different themes or theoretical concepts?		
	Are there clear similarities and differences among those themes or theories?		

(continued)

Checklist of structuring approaches for literature reviews			
3	**Methodological approach**	yes	no
	Are there several main methodologies used in the field?		
	Are those methodologies obviously distinct from each other?		
4	**Combination approach**	yes	no
	Can these sources be grouped by more than one criterion?		
	Is it necessary to review the sources in depth by combining the above approaches?		

III. Identifying the characteristics of an effective literature review: An effective literature review fulfills multiple purposes. Check the following literature review and identify the roles of a good literature review.

[①] Combustion instability is always a challenge in the development of advanced propulsion engines. The mechanisms that cause combustion instability involve multi-physical and chemical processes. [②] In gas-phase combustion, the instability process is mainly affected by the incomplete fuel-air mixing, flame-vortex interaction, flame-acoustic interaction, flame-flame interaction and wall boundary condition. [③] While in the spray combustion, liquid atomization and droplet evaporation processes also affect the combustion instability by changing the droplet diameter distribution and evaporation rate. These processes usually happen simultaneously and interact with each other, making the study of spray combustion instability mechanisms very difficult.

[④] Large eddy simulation (LES) can predict the unsteady combustion process with good accuracy and affordable computational cost and is a powerful method to investigate the mechanisms of combustion instability. In the LES of combustion instability, the flame was usually treated as acoustically compact. [⑤] LES coupled with global or reduced chemical schemes could give reasonable agreements with experiments in the reproduction of combustion instability. [⑥] Franzelli et al. applied LES with a two-step reduced mechanism to investigate the lean partially premixed combustion instability in a model gas turbine combustor, and found that incomplete mixing and equivalence ratio fluctuation were the source of combustion instability.

⑦ The same conclusions were also got in the study of combustion instability in a real gas turbine combustor conducted by Hermeth et al. ⑧ Ghani et al. used LES to investigate the longitudinal and transverse combustion instability in a model combustor. The chemistry was calculated using a two-step reduced mechanism. Results showed that both longitudinal and transverse frequency modes predicted by the LES agreed well with experiments. Flame roll-up and mean flame brush deformation were the dominant mechanisms that caused the combustion instability. ⑨ Palies et al. performed LES of unstable lean premixed flames under acoustic perturbation in a model gas turbine burner, and the chemistry was calculated using a single-step reaction mechanism. Results showed that LES could give good reproduction of flame dynamics. Vortex roll-up and swirl number fluctuation were the main driving mechanisms. As the heat release rate distributions and flame positions couldn't be reproduced accurately by the global reaction scheme, the gain and phase predicted by the LES had obvious differences with the experimental results. ⑩ Han et al. performed LES of two interacting flames response to external acoustic forcing with a four-step chemical reaction mechanism. Results showed that LES could give a good reproduction of flame-flame interaction under acoustic perturbation.

⑪ In the spray combustion, the combustion instability is not only affected by the flame-vortex interaction and equivalence ratio fluctuation, but also affected by the droplet dynamics. ⑫ Tachibana et al. applied LES method to the study of spray combustion instability in an aero-engine combustor at high temperature and high pressure. The chemical reactions were described by a detailed mechanism including 1537 reactions and 274 chemical species. The peak frequency and flame structure predicted by the LES agreed well with the experimental results, but the amplitudes of pressure fluctuations still had significant differences with experiments. ⑬ The results showed that the fluctuation of flame surface area was the dominant instability mechanisms, which was similar to the conclusions in a lean premixed gas-phase combustion instability conducted by Huang et al. ⑭ Kitano et al. used LES with a two-step reduced kerosene mechanism to investigate the effect of droplet diameter on the spray combustion instability. Results showed that the droplet diameter had a limited effect on the instability frequency but had a significant effect on the oscillation amplitude. The pressure oscillation amplitudes reached the maximum value when the initial averaged droplet diameter is 18.1 μm and decreased when the droplet diameter increased or decreased. These differences were mainly caused by the different droplet evaporation rates.

Although some researches have been done to study the spray combustion instability, the mechanisms that drive the combustion instability are still not well understood. The objective of this paper is to investigate more complex instability mechanisms of swirl stabilized spray flame in an aero-engine combustor using fully compressible LES method. The combustor includes a swirler, secondary air holes, third air holes and cooling films, and operates at elevated inlet temperature (740 K) and pressure (20 bar). The effects of droplet diameter and wall boundary condition on the combustion instability are also explored. The paper is organized as follows. The numerical methods, experimental configuration and computational details are described in Section 2. Results and discussions are presented in Section 3. And some conclusions are made in Section 4.

(Adapted from "Large eddy simulations of spray combustion instability in an aero-engine combustor at elevated temperature and pressure" by Cheng, Y. Z. et al. in *Aerospace Science and Technology*, Vol. 108, 2021.)

Fill the corresponding serial number into the table.

	Functions	Serial number
1	To identify a suitable topic for research.	①
2	To identify relevant literature of the research topic.	
3	To get an idea of the main debates on the research topic.	
4	To understand the issues and problems involved in the research topic.	
5	To grasp the existing approaches and methods in the research field.	
6	To summarize the existing literature.	

IV. The paper below is an overview about artificial intelligence in medicine. Read it carefully and do the following exercises.

1. **Read the paper once, understand the structure and fill in the blanks (A–I) with the following subheadings. Note that each subheading may be used more than once.**

Results	Conclusions	Discussion	Introduction
Materials and Methods	Objective	Background	

2. **Read the paper again and fill in the blanks (1–10) with appropriate expressions in the table below. Change the form if necessary.**

on the contrary	launch
utilize	hence
employ	in addition
dichotomize into	involve
apart from	base on

Overview of Artificial Intelligence in Medicine

Abstract

A. ________:

Artificial intelligence (AI) is the term used to describe the use of computers and technology to simulate intelligent behavior and critical thinking comparable to a human being. John McCarthy first described the term AI in 1956 as the science and engineering of making intelligent machines.

B. ________:

This descriptive article gives a broad overview of AI in medicine, dealing with the terms and concepts as well as the current and future applications of AI. It aims to develop knowledge and familiarity of AI among primary care physicians.

C. ________:

PubMed and Google searches were performed using the key words "artificial intelligence". Further references were obtained by cross-referencing the key articles.

D. ________:

Recent advances in AI technology and its current applications in the field of medicine have been discussed in detail.

E. ________:

AI promises to change the practice of medicine in hitherto unknown ways, but many of its practical applications are still in their infancy and need to be explored and developed better. Medical professionals also need to understand and acclimatize themselves with these advances for better healthcare delivery to the masses.

Keywords: artificial intelligence, future of medicine, machine learning, neural networks, robots

F. ________

Alan Turing (1950) was one of the founders of modern computers and AI. The "Turing test" (1) ________ the fact that the intelligent behavior of a computer is the ability to achieve human level performance in cognition related tasks. The 1980s and 1990s saw a surge in interest in AI. Artificial intelligent techniques such as fuzzy expert systems, Bayesian networks, artificial neural networks, and hybrid intelligent systems were used in different clinical settings in healthcare. In 2016, the biggest chunk of investments in AI research were in healthcare applications compared with other sectors.

AI in medicine can (2) ________ two subtypes: virtual and physical. The virtual part ranges from applications such as electronic health record systems to neural network-based guidance in treatment decisions. The physical part deals with robots assisting in performing surgeries, intelligent prostheses for handicapped people, and elderly care.

The basis of evidence-based medicine is to establish clinical correlations and insights via developing associations and patterns from the existing database of information. Traditionally, we used to (3) ________ statistical methods to establish these patterns and associations. Computers learn the art of diagnosing a patient via two broad techniques—flowcharts and database approach.

The flowchart-based approach (4) _______ translating the process of history-taking, i.e. a physician asking a series of questions and then arriving at a probable diagnosis by combining the symptom complex presented. This requires feeding a large amount of data into machine-based cloud networks considering the wide range of symptoms and disease processes encountered in routine medical practice. The outcomes of this approach are limited because the machines are not able to observe and gather cues which can only be observed by a doctor during the patient encounter.

(5) _______, the database approach utilizes the principle of deep learning or pattern recognition that involves teaching a computer via repetitive algorithms in recognizing what certain groups of symptoms or certain clinical/radiological images look like. An example of this approach is the Google's artificial brain project (6) _______ in 2012. This system trained itself to recognize cats based on 10 million YouTube videos with efficiency improving by reviewing more and more images. After 3 days of learning, it could predict an image of a cat with 75% accuracy.

G. _______

PubMed and Google searches were performed using the key words "artificial intelligence". Further references were obtained by cross-referencing the key articles. An overview of different applications utilizing AI technologies currently in use or in development is described.

H. _______

A lot of AI is already (7) _______ in the medical field, ranging from online scheduling of appointments, online check-ins in medical centers, digitization of medical records, reminder calls for follow-up appointments and immunization dates for children and pregnant females to drug dosage algorithms and adverse effect warnings while prescribing multidrug combinations.

Radiology is the branch that has been the most upfront and welcoming to the use of new technology. Computers being initially used in clinical imaging for administrative work like image acquisition and storage to now becoming an indispensable component of the work environment with the origin of picture archiving and communication system. (8) _______, the false-positive diagnoses may distract the radiologist resulting in unnecessary work-ups. As suggested by a study, AI could provide substantial aid in radiology by not only labeling abnormal exams but also by identifying quick negative exams in computed tomographies, X-rays, magnetic resonance images especially in high volume settings, and in hospitals with less available human resources.

A decision support system known as DXplain was developed by the university of Massachusetts in 1986, which gives a list of probable differentials based on the symptom complex and it is also used as an educational tool for medical students filling the gaps not explained in standard textbooks. Apart from that, the spectrum of AI has expanded to provide therapeutic facilities as well. AI-therapy is an online course that helps patients treat their social anxiety using therapeutic approach of cognitive behavior therapy. It was developed from a program CBTpsych.com at University of Sydney.

(9) ________ the inventions which already exist, there are certain advances in various phases of development, which will help physicians be better doctors. IBM's Watson Health being a prime example of the same, which will be equipped to efficiently identify symptoms of heart disease and cancer. Molly is a virtual nurse that is being developed to provide follow-up care to discharged patients allowing doctors to focus on more pressing cases.

I. ________

AI is growing into the public health sector and is going to have a major impact on every aspect of primary care. Primary care physicians can use AI to take their notes, analyze their discussions with patients, and enter required information directly into EHR systems. These applications will collect and analyze patient data and present it to primary care physicians alongside insight into patient's medical needs.

A study conducted in 2016 found that physicians spent 27% of their office day on direct clinical face time with their patients and spent 49.2% of their office day on electronic hospital records and desk work. When in the examination room with patients, physicians spent 52.9% of their time on EHR and other work. In conclusion, the physicians who used documentation support such as dictation assistance or medical scribe services engaged in more direct face time with patients than those who did not use these services. In addition, increased AI usage in medicine not only reduces manual labor and frees up the primary care physician's time but also increases productivity, precision, and efficacy.

Searching and developing pharmaceutical agents against a specific disease via clinical trials take years and cost a gazillion dollars. To quote a recent example, AI was used to screen existing medications, which could be used to fight against the emerging Ebola virus menace which would have taken years to process otherwise. With the help of AI, we would be able to embrace the new concept of "precision medicine".

Some studies have been documented where AI systems were able to outperform dermatologists in correctly classifying suspicious skin lesions. This because AI systems can learn more from successive cases and can be exposed to multiple cases within minutes, which far outnumber the cases a clinician could evaluate in one mortal lifetime. AI-based decision-making approaches are used in situations where experts often disagree, such as identifying pulmonary tuberculosis on chest radiographs.

This new era of AI-augmented practice has an equal number of skeptics as proponents. The increased utilization of technology has reduced the number of job opportunities, which many doctors in the making and practicing doctors are concerned about. Analytically and logically machines may be able to translate human behavior, but certain human traits such as critical thinking, interpersonal and communication skills, emotional intelligence, and creativity cannot be honed by the machines.

In 2016, the Digital Mammography DREAM Challenge was done where several networks of computers were connected, and the goal was to establish an AI-based algorithm by reviewing 640,000 digital mammograms. The best which was achieved was a specificity of 0.81, sensitivity of 0.80, area under receiver operator curve was 0.87, which is roughly approximated to bottom 10% radiologists. In conclusion, AI has potential, but it is unlikely that AI will replace doctors out rightly.

AI would be an integral part of medicine in the future. (10) ________, it is important to train the new generation of medical trainees regarding the concepts and applicability of AI and how to function efficiently in a workspace alongside machines for better productivity along with cultivating soft skills like empathy in them.

In conclusion, it is important that primary care physicians get well versed with the future AI advances and the new unknown territory the world of medicine is heading toward. The goal should be to strike a delicate mutually beneficial balance between effective use of automation and AI and the human strengths and judgment of trained primary care physicians. This is essential because AI completely replacing humans in the field of medicine is a concern which might otherwise hamper the benefits which can be derived from it.

(Adapted from "Overview of artificial intelligence in medicine" by Amisha, M. P. et al. in *Journal of Family Medicine and Primary Care*, Vol. 8, No. 7, 2019.)

Project

Work in groups. You need to:

1. Collect the literature reviews in introduction section of 5 journal articles and 5 MA theses written by Chinese students in English.
2. Evaluate the literature reviews of these 10 articles/theses according to the checklist in Exercise Ⅱ.
3. Compare them and find out how to improve the literature reviews of the MA theses.
4. Discuss with your group members and prepare a report for presentation in class.

Checklist of a well-written literature review				
Items		Yes	No	Not necessary
1	**Functions**			
	Clarifying contributions			
	Providing theoretical framework			
	Putting forward theoretical reasons			

(continued)

Checklist of a well-written literature review				
Items		Yes	No	Not necessary
2	**Characteristics**			
	Frontier			
	Tools or materials			
	Coverage			
	Correlation			
	Coherence			
	Analyzing rather than stacking			
3	**Innovations**			
	Theoretical innovations			
	A new theory			
	A new concept			
	New evidence			

Unit 5

Methodological Descriptions

Part I
Introducing the Unit

The methodology or methods section of a paper explains what type of research work you did and how you did it, allowing readers to evaluate the reliability and validity of your paper. Essentially, the research methodology is the blueprint of a research or a study. It should include: the type of research you did, the approach of data gathering and data analysis, the tools or materials used in the research and your rationale for choosing these methods. In a dissertation or an academic paper, the section of methodology comes after the introduction and before the results, discussion and conclusion. A literature review or theoretical framework might be presented before the methodology section.

In this unit, we will read methodological descriptions from journal articles and conference papers to present the structure and content of a methodology section as well as learn about the methods applied in the research.

Part II
Reading for Expressions

Study the bold-faced expressions that are often used in the methodology section of a paper.

Introducing Research Participants/Subjects

- **The scope of this study is** heavy-duty truck emissions in the Beijing–Tianjin–Hebei region of China.
- **To solve the first question, this paper applies** the theoretical framework of Tropospheric Ultraviolet-Visible Model (TUV) **to** calculations of radiation in 231 cities in China.
- The initial sample **consisted of** 200 students, 75 of whom belonged to minority groups.

Describing Data Collection Methods

- The GDP, freight volume and new heavy-duty truck registration of Beijing **are from the database of** the National Bureau of Statistics of China (NBSC).
- This component **is** fully **compliant with** international standards.
- **Criteria for** selecting the variables **were as follows**: environmental effects, managerial efficiency and technological factors.

Stating Research Procedures

- **Prior to** data collection, the participants received an explanation of the project.
- Two groups of compositions **are used** in this experiment.
- Experimental equipment **mainly includes** automobile driving simulator for road safety.
- Aerobic test was conducted **according to** the following steps.
- The surface **measurement was conducted** from Nov. 19, 2012 to Jan. 15, 2013 at Baolian meteorological station (39°56′N, 116°17′E) in the urban area of Beijing.
- **Before** stirring **continuously**, the medium **was maintained** at a temperature of 40 °C for 6h.

Conducting Data Analysis

- To model the dynamics of the planet–moon system, **we assume that** the FFP has been ejected from its host system.
- **To limit error accumulation**, when the mobile unit detects a signal, the position of the user **is updated** to the center of the zone.
- **Therefore**, the related trajectories of these trucks **were excluded from** the calculation.
- Analysis **was based on** the conceptual framework proposed by Smith et al.
- **Statistical analysis was performed** using SPSS software (version 20).
- **The data gathered** by the sensors **are processed by** the monitoring computer using an inertial localization algorithm.

Addressing Ethical Considerations

- **After approval of** the ethics committee (HADYEK-41) the study was performed **within the frame of rules specified by** the National Institute for animal experiments.
- Written **informed consent was obtained from** each enrolled patient.

Part III
Reading for Ideas

Passage A

Pre-reading tasks:

1. What is the main purpose of the methodology section?
2. How can we present the methods in a scientific way?

The Purpose of the Methodology Section

In the first section of the paper, the introduction, you should have stated the methodology employed in the study. If necessary, you also defended the reasons for your choice of a particular method over competing methods.

Now, in "Materials and Methods" (also designated in some cases by other names, such as "Experimental Procedures"), you must give the full details. Most of this section should be written in the past tense. The main purpose of the materials and methods section is to describe (and if necessary, defend) the experimental design and then provide enough detail so that a competent worker can repeat the experiments. Other purposes include providing information that will let readers judge the appropriateness of the experimental methods (and thus the probable validity of the findings) and that will permit assessment of the extent to which the results can be generalized. Many (probably most) readers of your paper will skip this section, because they already know from the introduction the general methods you used, and they probably have no interest in the experimental detail. However, careful writing of this section is critically important because the cornerstone of the scientific method requires that your results, to be of scientific merit, must be reproducible; and, for the results to be adjudged reproducible, you must provide the basis for repetition of the experiments by others. That experiments are unlikely to be reproduced is beside the point; the potential for reproducing the same or similar results must exist, or your paper does not represent good science.

When your paper is subjected to peer review, a good reviewer will read the materials and methods section carefully. If there is serious doubt that your experiments could be repeated, the reviewer will recommend rejection of your manuscript no matter how awe-inspiring your results.

(Adapted from *How to Write and Publish a Scientific Paper* by Gastel, B. & Day, R. A., Westport: Greenwood Press, 2016.)

Fill in the blanks:

The methods section is the most important part of a scientific paper because it provides the essential information that allows the reader to judge the (1) _______ of the results and (2) _______ of the study reported. Therefore, in this section the authors should describe the experimental (3) _______ and permit (4) _______ of the extent to which the results can be (5) _______. How to evaluate whether the methodology is (6) _______? It should be written in a clear and concise manner, but always present (7) _______ information so that the experiments could be (8) _______ by other researchers.

Passage B

Pre-reading tasks:

1. In what way can the methodology section be well-structured?
2. What should be included when describing statistical analysis?

How to Write the Methodology Section

Methods

For methods the usual order of presentation is chronological. Obviously, however, related methods should be described together, and straight chronological order cannot always be followed. For example, even if a particular assay was not done until late in the research, the assay method should be described along with the other assay methods, not by itself in a later part of the materials and methods section.

Headings

The materials and methods section often has subheadings. To see whether subheadings would indeed be suitable—and, if so, what types are likely to be appropriate—look at analogous papers in your target journal. When possible, construct subheadings that "match" those to be used in the results section. The writing of both sections will be easier if you strive for internal consistency, and the reader will be able to grasp quickly the relationship of a particular method to the related results.

Measurements and Analyses

Be precise. Methods are similar to cookbook recipes. If a reaction mixture was heated, give the temperature. Questions such as "how" and "how much" should be precisely answered by the author and not left for the reviewer or the reader to puzzle over.

Statistical analyses are often necessary, but your paper should emphasize the data, not the statistics. Generally, a lengthy description of statistical methods indicates that the writer has recently acquired this information and believes that the readers need similar enlightenment. Ordinary statistical methods generally should be used without comment; advanced or unusual methods may require a literature citation. In some fields, statistical methods or statistical software customarily is identified at the end of the materials and methods section.

Need for References

In describing the methods of the investigations, you should give (or direct readers to) sufficient details so that a competent worker could repeat the experiments. If your method is new (unpublished), you must provide all of the needed details. If, however, the method has been published in a journal, the literature reference should be given. For a method well known to readers, only the literature reference is needed. For a method with which readers might not be familiar, a few words of description tend to be worth adding, especially if the journal in which the method was described might not be readily accessible.

If several alternative methods are commonly employed, it is useful to identify your method briefly as well as to cite the reference. For example, it is better to state "cells were broken by ultrasonic treatment as previously described" than to state "cells were broken as previously described".

(Adapted from *How to Write and Publish a Scientific Paper* by Gastel, B. & Day, R. A., Westport: Greenwood Press, 2016.)

Fill in the blanks:

Usually the methods are presented in a(n) (1) _______ order. In some cases, related methods should be (2) _______ together. (3) _______ are recommended to be included in the methods section, whose correspondence to those of related results would realize internal (4) _______. Statistical analyses are often (5) _______, in which data, instead of statistics, should be (6) _______. Use of ordinary statistical methods is generally described (7) _______ comment while application of advanced methods requires a literature (8) _______.

Part IV
Reading for Speaking

Read the methodological descriptions in the following two passages, and then discuss the questions in groups.

Passage A

Understanding the Rising Phase of the $PM_{2.5}$ Concentration Evolution in Large China Cities

Methods

- **Air Pollutants Observations**

Hourly $PM_{2.5}$ observations in BJ, SH, and GZ are routinely monitored by the US embassy (or consulates). In BJ, the data set is available from 2008 to 2014. In SH and GZ, data are available from 2011 to 2014. The Tapered Element Oscillating Microbalance (TEOM) method was used to monitor $PM_{2.5}$ concentrations. Even though the data are not verified by embassy observers (consulates), they are in good agreement with observations by the China official monitoring network. Hourly concentrations of three gaseous pollutants, namely NO_2, CO, and SO_2, are monitored by the official monitoring network. The 2014 observation data were downloaded from the China National Urban Air Quality Real-time Publishing Platform, which is supported by the MEP (Ministry of Environment Protection). Their calibrations and quality controls are guaranteed by the China National Environmental Monitoring Center (CNEMC). The gaseous pollutants monitors, nearest to the $PM_{2.5}$ monitors in the US embassy or consulates, were used, namely NongZhanGuan in BJ, JingAn in SH, and TiYuGuan in GZ.

- **Meteorological Observations**

We used ground meteorological observations at the airports, ZBAA, HQAP and BYAP respectively in BJ, SH and GZ. The historical hourly meteorological observations were downloaded from the National Oceanic and Atmospheric Administration (NOAA) and the National Climatic Data Center (NCDC). The two meteorological variables used were wind speed and wind direction. These two variables are closely related to occurrence of $PM_{2.5}$ pollution processes.

- **Ground-Level $PM_{2.5}$ Concentrations**

To obtain $PM_{2.5}$ concentrations with improved spatial coverage, aerosol optical depth (AOD) retrieved from Moderate Resolution Imaging Spectroradiometer (MODIS) was always used as a proxy dataset. We used the ground-level $PM_{2.5}$ estimations in North China developed by Lv et al. The dataset provided us daily estimations with a complete spatial coverage in a Lambert Conic Conformal projection at a resolution of 12 km. The dataset time-span was from January 10th to December 31st, 2014.

- **24-hr Backward Trajectory Points**

Air mass trajectories provide a convenient and effective approach to evaluate pollutant transportation pathways. In this study, 24-hr air mass backward trajectory analysis was performed using the NOAA Hybrid Single Particle Lagrangian Integrated Trajectory (HYSPLIT-4) model. This model is widely used to calculate dispersion and air mass trajectories. The input meteorological data archive was obtained from the NCEP's Global Data Assimilation System (GDAS) with six-hr frequency. In the study, we modeled hourly 24-hr air mass backward points arriving at BJ (39.95°N, 116.47°E), SH (31.21°N, 121.44°E), and GZ (23.12°N, 113.32°E) to investigate pollution transport pathways. The arrival height was 200 m above the ground level. The 24-hr backward points in the hrs within the pollution hrs were extracted in each city.

(Adapted from "Understanding the rising phase of the $PM_{2.5}$ concentration evolution in large China cities" by Lv, B., Cai, J., Xu, B. & Bai, Y. in *Scientific Reports*, Vol. 7, 2017.)

Questions:

1. What air pollutants and meteorological variables are monitored during air pollutants observations and meteorological observations respectively?
2. The passage covers information about data collection of the study. Is this part precise and well-organized?

3. $PM_{2.5}$ is the primary pollutants in many cities worldwide while the pollution causes are not clearly understood. Take this study for example to discuss with your classmates contributions China has been making in resolving this issue. Have those Chinese authors cope with the issue in a scientific and reliable way? Can you find some supporting details from the passage?

Passage B

Designing Bioinspired Composite Reinforcement Architectures via 3D Magnetic Printing

Methods

- **Magnetic-Labeling of Reinforcing Particles**

Al_2O_3 (alumina) particles were kindly supplied by Antaria (Australia). The alumina particles are in platelet form with an average diameter of 7.5 μm and an average thickness of 350 nm. This provides an aspect ratio of around 21. To magnetize the alumina platelets, 375 μl of superparamagnetic iron oxide nanoparticles (SPIONS, EMG-705, 3.9% vol Fe_3O_4, Ferrotec, Bedford, NH, USA) was titrated with 10 g of Al_2O_3 in 200 ml of deionized water to ensure a homogenous coating of the microparticles. The mixture was stirred overnight using a magnetic stir bar. A negatively charged ligand-coating on the iron oxide allows the nanoparticles to electrostatically adsorb to the surface of the alumina particles. The particles are subsequently, filtered and dried. Once drying is complete, the magnetized alumina particles (m-Al_2O_3) were added to the photopolymer at desired volume fractions.

- **Preparation of Photopolymer-Ceramic Composite Resin**

UV-sensitive resin was made by first mixing aliphatic urethane diacrylate (Ebecryl 230) and isobornyl acrylate (IBOA, Sigma) in a 1:3 ratio by weight. Photo-initiators [phenylbis (2,4,6-trimethyl-benzoyl) phosphine oxide 97%, 1-Hydroxycyclohexyl phenyl ketone 99%] were added at 2% and 3% weight, and stirred overnight. The viscosity of the polymer blend was measured using an Ubbelohde viscometer (SimpleVIS, size 2C) and was found to be 140 mPa · s. Desired volume fractions of m-Al_2O_3 were added to the resin and were sonicated in volumes of 30 ml using a microtip sonifier (Branson 250, 20% duty cycle, 40 W output for

10 min) to ensure sufficient exfoliation. Finally, the resulting mixture was degassed to prevent bubbles from causing defects during the printing process.

- **3D Magnetic Printing Device**

The custom stereolithographic 3D printer used in this work utilizes an open-source software (Creation Workshop) to control a DLP projector (ViewSonic PJD7820hd) and two NEMA-17 stepper motors for the *z*-axis. The software's native slicing engine converts ".stl" files to a series of high-resolution vector files that are used to polymerize each cross section. The source files for this device are not limited to ".stl" files, and can also be generated directly from a ".jpeg, .tiff", and others. The printer's frame was purchased from mUVe 3D and modified to allow for the application of magnetic fields by either rotating a rare-earth magnet or using computer-controlled solenoids (4.5 in inner diameter, 2 in thick, 6 in outer diameter copper coil, Endicott Coil).

(Adapted from "Designing bioinspired composite reinforcement architectures via 3D magnetic printing" by Martin, J., Fiore, B. & Erb, R. in *Nature Communications*, Vol. 6, 2015.)

Questions:

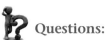

1. What is the working mechanism of the 3D printer used in this research?
2. The methods section is divided into three parts. How are they connected?
3. The experimental procedure is described with accompanied statements in brackets. Do you think it necessary to supply these statements? If yes, why? Discuss with your classmates whether the elements can be added in brackets in scientific paper writing.

Part V
Reading for Writing

I. **Based on Passage A and Passage B in "*Reading for Speaking*", which words (e.g. verbs, nouns) can be generally found in the methodology section? Can you find or think of any more words related to methodology writing? Add at least ten words to the list and share them with the class.**

Verbs	Nouns
provide	data
monitor	observation
…	…

II. **Methodology section includes data collection and analysis. Read Passage A in "*Reading for Speaking*" and write a brief summary with no less than 200 words that answers the following questions:**

- What data are included for study?
- How, where and when is the data collection conducted?
- Which kind of analysis or model is adopted for data analysis?

Exercises

I. Improve the following methodological descriptions in terms of wording, style and structure.

The apparatus for collecting electrocardiogram (ECG)'s consisted of the following: silver-silver chloride ECG electrodes (GE Medical Systems Silver Mactrode Plus Model E9001AD / Dymedix Dual Electrode Model 5200-0001), a differential amplifier (Isodam Biological B), an isolation amplifier (Texas Instruments ISO122) and a data acquisition (DAQ) board (Data Translation DT9804). The silver-silver chloride ECG electrodes were placed on the two wrists and left ankle.

After ECG recordings, the frequency response of the isolation amplifier is determined using a function generator (Wavetek). The difference of input (11.05 V) and output signal amplitude is measured on an oscilloscope (Hewlett Packard S4603B) as a function of frequency (which was varied from 0.65 Hz–2.35 kHz).

Aliasing effects are observed with the DAQ board by comparing input frequency (10-200 Hz signals from the Wavetek) and post-sampling observed frequencies using a 100 Hz sampling rate.

II. Read the following excerpt and then complete the exercises.

Methods

Study Design and Participants

This retrospective cohort study ***included*** two cohorts of adult inpatients (≥18 years old) from Jinyintan Hospital and Wuhan Pulmonary Hospital. All adult patients who were diagnosed with COVID-19 according to WHO interim guidance were screened, and those who died or were discharged between Dec 29, 2019 and Jan 31, 2020, ***were included*** in our study. Since these two hospitals were the only designated hospitals for transfer of patients with COVID-19 from other hospitals in Wuhan until Feb 1, 2020, our study ***enrolled*** all adult inpatients who were hospitalised for COVID-19 and had a definite outcome (dead or discharged) at the early stage of the outbreak.

Before Jan 11, 2020, SARS-CoV-2 RNA detection results were not available in the electronic medical records; therefore, this study ***includes*** 29 of the 41 patients originally reported on.

The study ***was approved*** by the Research Ethics Commission of Jinyintan Hospital and the requirement for ***informed consent*** was waived by the Ethics Commission.

Data Collection

Epidemiological, demographic, clinical, laboratory, treatment, and outcome data ***were extracted*** from electronic medical records using a standardized data collection form, which was a modified version of the WHO case record form for severe acute respiratory infections. All data ***were checked*** by two physicians (FZ and ZL) and a third researcher (GF) adjudicated any difference in interpretation between the two primary reviewers.

Laboratory Procedures

Methods for laboratory confirmation of SARS-CoV-2 infection ***have been described*** elsewhere. Briefly, four authority institutions were responsible for SARS-CoV-2 detection in respiratory specimens by next-generation sequencing or real-time RT-PCR methods. Throat-swab specimens ***were obtained*** for re-examination every other day after clinical remission of symptoms, including fever, cough, and dyspnoea, but only qualitative data were available. The ***criteria*** for discharge were absence of fever for at least 3 days, substantial improvement in both lungs in chest CT, clinical remission of respiratory symptoms, and two throat-swab ***samples*** negative for SARS-CoV-2 RNA obtained at least 24 h apart.

Routine blood examinations were complete blood count, coagulation profile, serum biochemical tests, myocardial enzymes, interleukin-6 (IL-6), serum ferritin, and procalcitonin. Chest radiographs or CT scan were also done for all inpatients. Frequency of examinations was determined by the treating physician.

Statistical Analysis

Continuous and categorical variables ***were presented*** as median (IQR) and n (%), respectively. We used the Mann-Whitney U test, X^2 test, or Fisher's exact test to ***compare*** differences between survivors and non-survivors where appropriate. To ***explore*** the risk factors associated with in-hospital death, univariable and multivariable logistic regression models were used. Considering the total number of deaths (n=54) in our study and to avoid overfitting in the model, five variables—lymphocyte count, d-dimer, SOFA score, coronary heart disease, and age—***were chosen*** for multivariable analysis on the basis of previous findings and clinical constraints.

We ***excluded*** variables from the univariable analysis if their between-group differences were not significant, if their accuracy was unconfirmed, if the number of events was too small to ***calculate*** odds ratios, and if they had colinearity with the SOFA score.

We ***compared*** patient characteristics between the two hospitals and used a generalized linear model to adjust for possible ***differences*** in patients' characteristics and treatment between the two study centers. A two-sided α of less than 0.05 ***was considered statistically significant***. Statistical analyses were done using the SAS software (version 9.4), unless otherwise indicated.

Role of the Funding Source

The funder of the study had no role in study design, data collection, data analysis, data interpretation, or writing of the report. The corresponding authors ***had full access to*** all the data in the study and had final ***responsibility*** for the decision to submit for publication.

(Adapted from "Clinical course and risk factors for mortality of adult inpatients with COVID-19 in Wuhan, China: A retrospective cohort study" by Zhou, F., Yu, T., Du, R. H. et al. in *Lancet*, Vol. 395, 2020.)

1. **Fill in the blanks with the italicized words or expressions from the text above. Change the form if necessary.**

 1) 29 of the 41 patients were ________ in our study.

 2) This study was equipped with ________ by the Research Ethics Commission.

 3) Data were ________ electronic medical records rendering into a standardized form.

4) The ________ for discharge were described as follows.

5) A series of tests were operated to ________ differences between patients.

6) Two models were used to ________ the risk factors associated with mortality.

2. Answer the following questions according to the text above.

1) What is the source of research data? What kind of processes do the data go through before statistical analysis?

2) What are the statistical test methods, variables, models adopted and software respectively?

3) A cohort usually refers to a group of people who share a common feature. So what is a retrospective cohort study based on the study design in this passage?

III. The following are taken from a methodology section. Put them in the correct order to form a meaningful narrative.

① Compared with traditional testing methods not keeping pace with large number of situations required for autonomous driving validation, this method is applied in simulated environments as well as runs and evaluates thousands of simulated scenarios autonomously.

② The simulation testing environments are based on real traffic environment with 3D data collection and modeling, as shown in Figure 7. The testing was firstly carried out in simulation environment achieved by mixed simulation testing methods. Then the driving test was performed in corresponding real environment.

③ Therefore, the simulation models of various components can be corrected with feedback, overcoming the problem of inaccuracy during simulation. This results from that the simulation environment can be easily reconstructed with scenario auto generation tools.

IV. The following is an abridged version of a research article. Analyze the text to understand the functions and structure of methodology in scientific writings.

1. Context: Software Engineering (SE) is an evolving discipline with new subareas being continuously developed and added. To structure and better understand the SE body of knowledge, (1)________ have been proposed in all SE knowledge areas.

2. Objective: The objective of this paper is to characterize the state-of-the-art research on SE taxonomies.

3. Research Methodology

We chose the systematic mapping study method (SMS) to (2)________ the state-of-the-art towards taxonomies in SE, because this method works well for broad and weakly defined research areas. We employed the guidelines by Kitchenham and Charters and partly implemented the mapping process provided by Petersen et al. The employed mapping process is summarized in Fig. 1 and described further in Subsections 3.1–3.4.

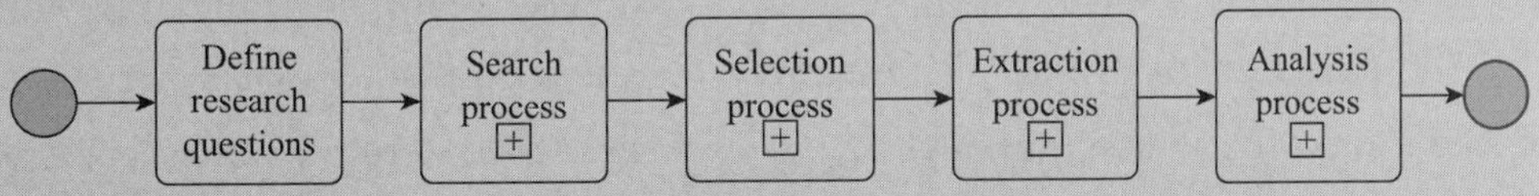

Fig. 1 Employed systematic mapping process.

3.1 Search Process

The search process employed in this work is explained in this subsection.

First, we defined the terms to be included in our search string. We selected all SWEBOK knowledge areas to be included as terms, except for the three knowledge areas on related disciplines (Computing Foundations, Mathematical Foundations and Engineering Foundations). We also included the term "Software Engineering", to (3)________ of the search string. Finally, to reduce the scope of the search string to studies that report SE taxonomies, we included the term "taxonomy". The final search string is shown below.

Once the search string was designed, we selected the primary sources to search for relevant studies. Scopus, Compendex/Inspec and Web of Science were selected because they cover most of the important SE databases, such as IEEE, Springer, ACM and Elsevier.

3.2 Study Selection Process

The selection process employed in this work is displayed as follows.

First, the following inclusion and exclusion criteria were defined.

- Inclusion criteria:

1. Studies that propose or extend a taxonomy AND
2. Studies that are within Software Engineering (SE), according to SWEBOK's KAs.

- Exclusion criteria:

1. Studies where the full-text is not accessible OR;
2. Studies that do not propose or extend a SE taxonomy OR;
3. Studies that are not written in English OR;
4. Studies that are not reported in a peer-reviewed workshop, conference, or journal.

The selection of primary studies was conducted using a two-stage screening procedure. In the first stage, only (4)________ were considered. In the second stage, the full texts were read. Note that we used in both stages an inclusive approach to avoid premature exclusion of studies, i.e. if there was doubt about a study, such a study was to be included.

3.3 Extraction Process

The extraction process employed in this work is summarized in Fig. 2 and consists of four main steps: Define a classification scheme, define an extraction form, extract data, and validate the extracted data.

We designed classification scheme by following Petersen et al.'s guidelines. It has the following facets: research type, SE knowledge area and presentation approach.

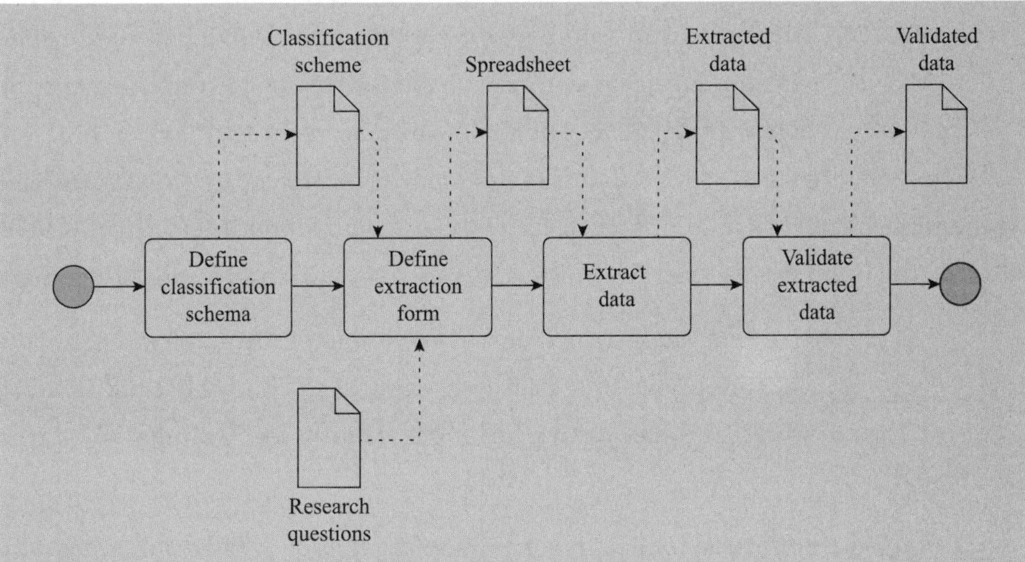

Fig. 2 Extraction process.

To improve (5)________, we decided to re-screen all 280 papers, focusing on the item "classification structure". The first step started with discussion over classification structures in detail (based on Kwasnik) to come to a common understanding of the terms. Next, three of us did an independent re-assessment of 52 papers. As a result, full agreement was reached on 50 papers (3 identical results) and partial agreement on 2 papers (2 reviewers agreeing). There were no primary studies without full or partial agreement. Third, the remaining 228 studies were re-assessed by the first and second authors and they reached agreement on 216 papers. The remaining 12 papers were independently re-assessed by the third author. In the end, full agreement was achieved for 50 studies and partial agreement was achieved for 230 studies.

During (6)________, 10 studies were excluded because they do not present taxonomies, reducing the final number of primary studies to 270.

3.4 Analysis Process

To begin with, we classified the extracted data using the scheme defined in Subsection 3.3. This led to the results detailed in Section 4 Results. (7)________ was also performed to answer the research questions of this paper. Finally, the overall result of the data analysis (see Section 4), along with information from additional literature, was used to revise an existing method previously proposed to design SE taxonomies.

4. Results: An increasing number of SE taxonomies have been published since 2000 in a broad range of venues. The majority of taxonomies can be grouped into the following SWEBOK knowledge areas: construction (19.55%), design (19.55%), requirements (15.50%) and maintenance (11.81%). (8)________ (45.76%) is the most frequently used approach for taxonomy validation. Hierarchy (53.14%) and faceted analysis (39.48%) are the most frequently used classification structures.

5. Conclusion: There is a strong interest in taxonomies in SE, but few taxonomies are (9)________. Taxonomy design decisions regarding the used classification structures, procedures and descriptive bases are usually not well described and motivated.

(Adapted from "Taxonomies in software engineering: A systematic mapping study and a revised taxonomy development method" by Usman, M., Britto, R., Börstler, J. & Mendes, E. in *Information and Software Technology*, Vol. 85, 2017.)

1. **Read the article and fill in the blanks with the following words or expressions. Change the form if necessary.**

A. extend or revise

B. the abstracts and titles of the studies

C. the reliability of the extracted data

D. illustrate

E. augment the comprehensiveness

F. identify and analyze

G. the re-assessment of the primary studies

H. a quantitative analysis of the extracted data

I. taxonomies

2. **Read the following descriptions about methodology. Judge whether the statements are true or false.**

	Descriptions about methodology	True	False
1	Without strong methodological foundations, the results will lack reliability, which hinders researchers' capacity to discuss the implications of research.		

(continued)

	Descriptions about methodology	True	False
2	Appropriate subheadings help organize the methods section.		
3	When using a method proposed by other researchers, citation is not necessary.		
4	In general, the description of procedures and measurements should be organized chronologically.		
5	The methods section is always written in the present tense.		
6	Methods should be designed to answer research questions.		
7	When describing data collection, only sources of data should be included.		
8	Some details can be neglected even if other researchers are not able to replicate or adapt the study after omission.		
9	Data analysis focuses on information on how the author intends to analyze the data instead of the results of analysis.		
10	Although the methods cannot be perfect, limitations should not be stated in the paper.		

Project

Work in groups. You need to:

1. Collect the methods section of 5 top journal articles and 5 MA theses written by Chinese students in English.
2. Evaluate the methods section of these 10 articles/theses according to the checklist below.
3. Compare them and find out how to improve the methodology part of the MA theses.
4. Discuss with your group members and prepare a report for presentation in class.

Checklist of a well-written methodology section				
	Items	Yes	No	Not necessary
1	**Content**			
	Research design			
	Participants/samples/subjects			
	Data selection criteria			
	Data collection			
	Data analysis			
	Tools or materials			
	Experiment procedures			
	Comparison with previous methods			
	Limitations			
	Ethical considerations			
	Funding statement			
2	**Wording/Style**			
	Past tense			
	Academic expressions			
	Clarity			
	Subheadings			
	Well-structured/logical order			
	Sufficient details to repeat the study			

Unit 6

Results and Discussion

Part I
Introducing the Unit

This unit will guide you to analyze the section of results and discussion. The results section of a research paper is where findings are reported as a result of the methodology applied. Results should simply state the findings and arrange them in a logical sequence, without bias or interpretation. The discussion part should interpret and describe the significance of research findings in light of the research questions being investigated, and explain the new understanding of or fresh insights into the problem. We can find the answers to the research questions and evaluate the robustness of the research findings.

In this unit, excerpts from journal articles are given to help you understand how results and discussion are presented.

Part II
Reading for Expressions

Study the bold-faced expressions that are often used in the results and discussion section of a paper.

Describing the Research Design

- **This study sought to comprehensively evaluate** the Grassland Ecological Compensation Policy (GECP) program **based on its stated objectives**.
- **Our data covers** a total of 1037 coal plants, nearly 3000 individual units, operating in China.
- **These data reflect the success of** China's policy goal of decreasing low-grade scrap imports.

Presenting Results

- **On average**, Normalized Difference Vegetation Index (NDVI) increased by 1.2% in GECP regions from the pre-program period (2006—2010) to the program period (2011—2015).
- **Figure 1 also indicates** that NDVI increased in some areas and decreased in other areas.
- **Figure 3a addresses** the skill distributions over six major occupational groups.
- **Descriptive information** on the number of deaths by cause and individual characteristics **is presented** in Table 3.

Analyzing Results

- **Multiple analyses were conducted** to test **the robustness of** the main results.
- Here we **compare the results of** the proposed method **with** those of the traditional methods.
- **The optimization is carried out** over a time window of 400 days, roughly **corresponding to** the duration of a simulated epidemic with no vaccination.
- To **strategize** the phaseout of all the coal plants, we first conduct a systematic evaluation.

- **We have studied** the essential nature of power electronic converters based on communication theory and **established an analogy** between the operation principles of power electronics and communications.

Interpretating Results

- This **suggests** that improvements should be made to enhance the program's effect on both grassland quality and herder livelihood.
- Increased risk of headache **was correlated with** MP use.
- **It must be taken into consideration that** when the consumers' demands increase, the pressure on the healthcare providers also increases.
- **In line with previous work**, we found that differences between prioritization strategies are negligible when the daily capacity is high enough.
- **These findings are inconsistent with** several previous studies.
- **This novel finding is likely associated with** the methodology we used, which allowed us to consider strategies where the vaccination can target a new age group before the full coverage in the previous group is reached.
- **To properly interpret our findings**, it is important to consider the limitations of the performed analysis.
- This fundamental research **offers a new perspective on** power electronics.

Part III
Reading for Ideas

Passage A

Pre-reading tasks:

1. What are supposed to be included in the results section?
2. How can we achieve clarity in the results section?

How to Write the Results Section

Content of the Results

So now we come to the core of the paper, the data. This part of the paper is called the results section.

Contrary to popular belief, you shouldn't start the results section by describing methods that you inadvertently omitted from the materials and methods section.

There are usually two ingredients of the results section. First, you should give some kind of overall description of the experiments, providing the big picture without repeating the experimental details previously provided in materials and methods. Second, you should present the data. Your results should be presented in the past tense. Of course, it isn't quite that easy. How do you present the data? A simple transfer of data from laboratory notebook to manuscript will hardly do.

Most importantly, in the manuscript you should present representative data rather than endlessly repetitive data. The fact that you could perform the same experiment 100 times without significant divergence in results might be of considerable interest to your major professor, but editors, not to mention readers, prefer a little bit of predigestion. Aaronson (1977, p.10) said it another way: "The compulsion to include everything, leaving nothing out, does not prove that one has unlimited information; it proves that one lacks discrimination." Exactly the same concept, and it is an important one, was stated almost a century earlier by John Wesley Powell, a geologist who served as president of the American Association for the Advancement of Science in 1888. In Powell's words: "The fool collects facts; the wise man selects them."

Strive for Clarity

The results should be short and sweet, without verbiage. Mitchell (1968) quoted Einstein as having said, "If you are out to describe the truth, leave elegance to the tailor." Although the results section is the most important part, it is often the shortest, particularly if it is preceded by a well-written materials and methods section and followed by a well-written discussion.

The results need to be clearly and simply stated because it is the results that constitute the new knowledge that you are contributing to the world. The earlier parts of the paper (introduction, materials and methods) are designed to tell why and how you got the results; the later part of the paper (discussion) is designed to tell what they mean. Obviously, therefore, the whole paper must stand or fall on the basis of the results. Thus, the results must be presented with crystal clarity.

(Adapted from *How to Write and Publish a Scientific Paper* by Gastel, B. & Day, R. A., Westport: Greenwood Press, 2016.)

Fill in the blanks:

There are usually two (1) ________ of the results section. First, a(n) (2) ________ description of the experiments should be given without (3) ________ details previously provided in the methods section. Second, (4) ________ are supposed to be presented in past tense. How to present the data? Most importantly, (5) ________ data rather than endlessly repetitive data should be presented. Tables and graphs can be supplemented to present data. To achieve (6) ________, the results should be stated (7) ________ and simply because this part (8) ________ new knowledge on which the whole paper stand.

Passage B

Pre-reading tasks:

1. What are supposed to be included in the discussion section?
2. How do results and discussion correspond to the remaining parts of a paper?

Components of the Discussion

What are the essential features of a good discussion? The main components will be provided if the following injunctions are heeded.

a. Try to present the principles, relationships, and generalizations shown by the results. And bear in mind, in a good discussion, you discuss—you do not recapitulate—the results.

b. Point out any exceptions or any lack of correlation and define unsettled points. Never take the high-risk alternative of trying to cover up or fudge data that do not quite fit.

c. Show how your results and interpretations agree (or contrast) with previously published work.

d. Don't be shy; discuss the theoretical implications of your work, as well as any possible practical applications.

e. State your conclusions as clearly as possible.

f. Summarize your evidence for each conclusion. Or, as the wise old scientist will tell you, "Never assume anything except a 4-percent mortgage."

Much as the methods and the results should correspond to each other, the introduction and the discussion should function as a pair. At least implicitly, the introduction should have posed one or more questions. The discussion should indicate what the findings say about the answers. Failure to address the initial questions commonly afflicts discussions. Be sure the discussion answers what the introduction asked.

Whereas the content of the introduction commonly moves from the general topic to your specific research, in sort of a funnel format, the discussion tends to do largely the reverse, much like an inverted funnel. For example, a well-structured discussion may first restate the main findings, then discuss how they relate to findings of previous research, then note implications and applications, and perhaps then identify unanswered questions well suited for future research.

In the introduction, you invited readers into your research venue; in the discussion, you usher them out, now well informed about your research and its meaning.

(Adapted from *How to Write and Publish a Scientific Paper* by Gastel, B. & Day, R. A., Westport: Greenwood Press, 2016.)

Fill in the blanks:

The primary purpose of the discussion section is to show the (1) ________ and generalizations among observed facts. (2) ________ should be stated as clearly as possible with support of evidence. Any (3) ________ or any lack of correlation and unsettled points ought to be pointed out. Much as the methods and the results should (4) ________ to each other, the introduction and the discussion should function as a(n) (5) ________. The discussion should indicate and answer the (6) ________ proposed in introduction. Whereas the introduction commonly moves from the general topic to (7) ________ research, the discussion tends to do largely the reverse by giving (8) ________ and applications of the research.

Part IV
Reading for Speaking

Read the results and discussion in the following two passages, and then discuss the questions in groups.

Passage A

Direction Change of Redirected Walking via a Single Shoe Height Change

Results and discussion

Among the 20 participants, the first two participants had light leakage problems in their head-mounted displays. They didn't lean to either side under normal conditions, and they kept going straight throughout the experiment. After that, we used the nose pad for the Helmet-Mounted Displays (HMD), and the situation was improved. Among the remaining 18 participants, they walked 5 times in the virtual environment with normal shoes. 9 of them tended to lean to the left, and 9 participants tended to the right. The data of participants showed that the probability of turning in the opposite direction as the shoe height increases in the experiment has nothing to do with the participant's leg length.

The biggest found of the paper was that as the height difference between the two shoes increased, the probability and angle of the participant's turning in the opposite direction also increased. For example, P13 (Left foot height changed and shoes height changed from low to high) tended to walk in an arc to the right when he is wearing shoes of normal height in the virtual environment. As the height difference between the two shoes increases, he tended to walk in an arc to the left. Figure 3 shows the results of the experiment. The probability's calculation formula is shown in Figure 4.1.

In terms of user experience, the 5-level Likert scale was used to represent the comfort of the shoes. 0 is no feeling, 4 is very serious discomfort. When the height difference between two shoes was less than 0.6cm, the participant had little discomfort with the height of shoes. When the height of a shoe increases, the discomfort perceived by the participants increases with the height. However, when the height difference between the two shoes decreased from high to low, the participants' discomfort with their feet showed an overall downward trend, but the fluctuation was small. Finally, comparison by means of a paired-sample two-tailed *t*-test revealed a significant difference between the overall simulator sickness scores obtained before and after exposure to the virtual environment ($t_{(20)} = -2.691$, $p<0.05$). Average total SSQ score of participants before the experiment is about 65.2026, but the average total SSQ score of participants after the experiment is about 218.8274. It showed that the experiment can be carried out normally without notable simulator sickness.

(Adapted from "Direction change of redirected walking via a single shoe height change" by Zhang, Y. & Hong, J. in *2021 IEEE Conference on Virtual Reality and 3D User Interfaces Abstracts and Workshops (VRW)*,2021.)

 Questions:

1. What is the biggest finding of this paper?
2. Paragraph 1 provides an overall description of the experiment which has been thoroughly introduced in the methods section. Do you think it necessary to present it again in the results section? Why?

3. This passage has included the review of experiment, representative data, statistical analysis, major findings, etc. However, there is still room for improvement. What do you think can be improved?

Passage B

Impact of Artificial Light at Night on Diurnal Plant–Pollinator Interactions

Results and discussion

This study highlights the complex ways in which artificial illumination can affect visual ecology. By comprehensively modelling the effects of light emission spectra, light intensity, surface reflectance and receiver vision we have revealed a range of previously unforeseen relationships. The most striking finding is that broadband amber light sources (such as PC amber LEDs and high pressure sodium) are predicted to have a disruptive effect on hawkmoth flower colour perception. At high intensities these light sources can provide very good colour discrimination for finding flowers, however, under lower intensities (typically found tens of meters from a light source, or under skyglow) the same light source can actually inhibit colour discrimination. This is likely to interfere with a hawkmoth's ability to remember and efficiently handle flowers. Narrow-band sources (such as LPS and orange LED) prevent perception of colour contrasts in moth wings and between flowers and vegetation, and may result in poor background resting location choices, leaving the moths more vulnerable to diurnal predators.

A variety of approaches to reducing the environmental impact of artificial nighttime lighting have been proposed. In the main, these concern quite generic changes to reduce the spatial and temporal occurrence of such lighting, to limit its intensity and to limit the use of broader spectrum and blue-rich lighting. Animal visual ecology is an increasingly important factor in these recommendations, as recent evidence from comparisons between emission spectra of artificial lights and behavioural responses or spectral sensitivities of different species suggest that broad-spectrum lights are most likely to disrupt ecological interactions. By contrast, amber LEDs have been seen as less harmful, and are being deployed with, still low but, increasing frequency. This approach is based on a range of mechanisms, notably observations of insect phototaxis that show high capture rates in light traps with high blue/UV output, and fitted models that suggest that the UV and blue photoreceptors in insects are key in driving phototaxis, as well as the effects of blue-rich light in suppressing melatonin production across a wide range of taxa. However, artificial nighttime lighting can interfere with insect ecology in a wide variety of ways, and potential solutions for one problem may be inappropriate for others. For example, narrow-band long-wavelength lighting may reduce interference with bioluminescent signals, such as those of some fireflies, but inhibit perception of colour signals by other insects. More comprehensive assessments of the effects of spectral composition of light sources on visual ecology, and hence on aspects of behaviour such as foraging, predation rates, and mate selection have not previously been undertaken. The results reported here, suggesting previously under-appreciated effects of amber lighting on the visual ecology of valuable nocturnal pollinators, argue for more in-depth assessments of the impacts of specific lights on relevant ecological interactions, and a more nuanced approach to solutions for mitigation.

(Adapted from "Impact of artificial light at night on diurnal plant–pollinator interactions" by Giavi, S., Fontaine, C. & Knop, E. in *Nature Communications,* Vol. 12, 2021.)

Questions:

1. What are the effects of broadband amber light sources on hawkmoth? Do these sources at different light intensities exert similar effects?
2. This article has been structured following the principle of internal consistency. The discussion section responds to the research questions proposed in introduction one after another. Can you infer the two research questions according to the content of discussion section?
3. Human activities have significantly affected ecosystems. In this passage, effects of artificial lighting on insects are investigated and possible solutions are discussed. What are the solutions proposed by those authors? How do they verify their advantages over other approaches?

Part V
Reading for Writing

The results section reports representative data of the research design while the discussion section answers research questions based on the results. Read Passage B in "Reading for Speaking" and write a brief summary with no less than 200 words that answers the following questions:

- What are the major findings of this study?
- What approach has been proposed to solve the problem discussed in this paper?
- What can be further studied about this topic?

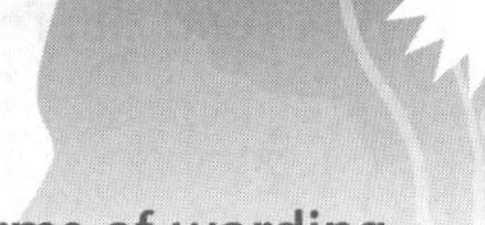

Exercises

I. Improve the following results and discussion section in terms of wording, style and structure.

Results

More green material is removed by the finches than red, more red than black and more black than orange. The ratio between material of different colors used in nest construction differed significantly with the expected 1:1:1:1 (X^2=63.44, df=3, p<.005). When colors were compared in pairs, the difference between values for green and red were not significantly different (X^2=117, df=1, p>.5). Similarly, the values for black and orange were significantly different (X^2=36.38, df=1, p<.005).

Discussion

The results from these experiments suggest that zebra finches do in fact have color preferences with regard to nesting material. Contrary to the predictions made by specifying Burley's studies (1981, 1982), the zebra finches used in this study preferred green, red or black nesting material to orange. These results are similar to those of Collias (1981) who show that weaver birds preferred green nesting material.

It is possible that zebra finches prefer green material to red, black and orange. The reason is that green is more similar to the color of the grasses commonly used as nesting material in their natural environment. This interpretation, however, does not explain the preference for red and black materials over orange.

Alternatively, it is not possible that the strong preference shown for green material may be a result of imprinting on the color of the nests they grew up in. It has been shown, for example, that parental plumage color has a strong effect on mate selection in male (but not female) zebra finches (Walter, 1973). All of the birds used in this study have exposed to grass, green embroidery floss and white dog fur in nests.

II. Read the following excerpt and then complete the exercises.

4. Results

We ***collected*** 3090 real world clinical cases made by famous elder TCM masters from literatures in Chinese Knowledge Center for Engineering Science and Technology (CKCEST). ***As an example***, a clinical case is shown in Fig. 3. It ***describes*** the patient's chief complaint and history, how a doctor diagnoses and prescribes and the doctor's remark on the case. Texts ***marked*** red are ***identified as*** symptoms in TCM ontology, and texts marked blue are herbal medicines in *TCM MeSH* which form a prescription.

4.1 Experimental results

Syndrome Labeling. We now show the syndrome labeling and treatment method determining result. Taking the clinical case in Fig. 3 as an example, the symptoms marked red are ***mapped to*** syndromes "interior heat syndrome", "wind syndrome" and "syndrome of blood stasis" with map count 2, 5 and 5 ***respectively***, which means 2 of them are in "interior heat syndrome" category, 5 of them are in "wind syndrome" category and 5 of them are in "syndrome of blood stasis" category. They are selected as syndrome labels with map probability larger than the threshold. After labeling syndromes, the treatment methods "heat-clearing", "wind-relieving" and "blood-regulating" ***are determined by*** syndrome-treatment method connection in TCM ontology, as shown in Fig. 4, which is quite close to the real situation in this case.

Topic discovering. The 23 topics learned from the clinical cases are shown in Table 1, Table 2, Table 3, Table 4. We show top ten herbal medicines with posterior probability in each topic. Most of them (92.17%) can be ***validated*** in *TCM MeSH* and TCM textbooks, italicized medicines are not in prescriptions of corresponding function category in *TCM MeSH* and textbooks. We can see most of the medicines are validated, others (italicized) could be useful complements to the categories or used together with medicines in the corresponding function category.

Function Prediction. Table 5 shows the classification performance. From the table, we can see that SVM and Bayes Network produce the highest F-Measure scores among 6 classifiers, and Bayes Network achieves the highest F-Measure score

0.5113 on the combined feature space. When using medicine vector features, the result is not good, only SVM and Bayes Network ***perform relatively well***. When utilizing topics features, ***high precision can be achieved***, but the recall is not satisfactory, which means the posterior probability can ***highlight*** the most possible treatment methods labels, but ***ignores*** other labels. When combining the two feature spaces, the ***predictive abilities*** of functions (treatment methods) are improved over medicine features. For F-Measure, the improvement is statistically significant by a 2-tailed paired *t*-test at 95% confidence under all classifiers. The treatment patterns are validated, and can be ***exploited*** to understand the TCM clinical data better.

4.2 Discussion

From experimental results, we can see that our method can ***automatically*** label TCM clinical cases by syndrome labels, which is useful for clinical case ***classification and organization***; our method can discover medicine usage patterns from a large number of clinical records for each syndrome, which is helpful for summarizing experiences of TCM doctors; our method can improve prescription function prediction by using medicine co-occurrence information rather than using medicines only, which could provide some suggestions for prescribing. However, our method has some ***limitations*** and could be improved.

In syndrome labeling step, we simply use text matching to identify symptoms and medicines. This is a naive approach, which could be improved by named entity recognition and entity linking.

It is possible to set the number of topics to a number different from the number of unique treatment methods by using more sophisticated partially supervised topic models.

Although we can improve the function prediction performance by using topic features, the result is not very satisfactory. The performance could be improved further by considering medicine information in TCM knowledge. For instance, we can use medicine's function class and description in *TCM MeSH* as features. ***Additionally***, we can also utilize the dosage of each medicine in a prescription.

Our *framework* can be directly applied to analyze ***large scale*** TCM clinical cases in hospitals. The labeling process and topic model could be easily ***parallelized*** in MapReduce.

(Adapted from "Discovering treatment pattern in Traditional Chinese Medicine clinical cases by exploiting supervised topic model and domain knowledge" by Yao, L., Zhang, Y., Wei, B. G. et al. in *Journal of Biomedical Informatics*, Vol. 58, 2015.)

1. Fill in the blanks with the italicized words or expressions from the text above. Change the form if necessary.

1) Given a collection of TCM clinical cases, symptoms and medicines were ________ and ________ with different colors.

2) After ________ symptoms in a clinical case to syndromes, the treatment methods will be determined.

3) Results of function prediction varied when utilizing different ________ such as medicine vector, topics or their combination.

4) The method is useful for clinical case classification and organization through ________ labeling.

5) ________ in each experimental process and corresponding solutions have been proposed.

6) Function prediction performance can be improved by taking into ________ medicine information and dosage of each medicine.

2. Answer the following questions according to the text above.

1) Please list some syndrome labels used in this study. Why are they selected as syndrome labels?

2) What is the structure of 4.2 Discussion?

3) According to the authors, the framework in this paper can be directly applied to analyze large scale TCM clinical cases in hospitals. Can you summarize its advantages?

III. The following are taken from a discussion section. Put them in the correct order to form a meaningful narrative.

① In summary, the NHSC study has provided valuable data not only with regard to indicators of health outcomes but also on diet, lifestyle and genetic factors. The NHSC study is expected to determine the interactions of these factors in the development of NCDs and to provide further insights into the underlying mechanisms.

② Several limitations should be mentioned. First, attrition is a concern. Although we have made efforts to retain cohort participants, the response rates have decreased over time in common with most cohort studies. Second, as people who are concerned with their health are more likely to participate in the study, we could not rule out the possibility of healthy volunteer bias.

③ The NHSC is a longitudinal open cohort study with broad research aims. The major advantages include its random sampling with a relatively large sample size, long duration of follow-up, detailed and repeated assessments of sociodemographical characteristics, dietary intake, and lifestyle practices as well as the use of comprehensive biochemical markers to characterize health outcomes.

IV. The following is an abridged version of a research article. Analyze the text to understand the functions and structure of the results and discussion part in scientific writings.

1\. **Context:** Information visualization is paramount for the analysis of Big Data. The volume of data requiring interpretation is continuously growing. However, users are usually not experts in information visualization. Thus, defining the visualization that best suits a determined context is a very challenging task for them. Moreover, it is often the case that users do not have a clear idea of what objectives they are building the visualizations for. Consequently, it is possible that graphics are misinterpreted, making wrong decisions that lead to missed opportunities. One of the (1)________ in this process is the lack of methodologies and tools that non-expert users in visualizations can use to define their objectives and visualizations.

2. Objective: The main objectives of this paper are to (i) enable non-expert users in data visualization to communicate their analytical needs with little effort, (ii) generate the visualizations that best fit their requirements, and (iii) evaluate the impact of our proposal (2)________ a case study, describing an experiment with 97 non-expert users in data visualization.

3. Methods: We propose a methodology that collects user requirements and semi-automatically creates suitable visualizations. Our proposal (3)________ the whole process, from the definition of requirements to the implementation of visualizations. The methodology has been tested with several groups to measure its effectiveness and perceived usefulness.

4. Results and Discussion

4.1 Experimental Results

After manually transcribing the survey, the analytical questions, and the rubric for a subsequent analysis, we obtained the results shown in Table 6. We have (4)________ the results in:

- Group 123: 45 college computer engineering students who were assisted while carrying out the experiment.

According to the results obtained, shown in Table 6, the set of visualizations generated without following any methodology can answer 1.87/4 (47%) of the specific questions proposed, while this number grows until 2.72/4 (68%) coverage when following the proposed method. Furthermore, a 2-Sample T-Test was performed with an alpha of 0.05. Thanks to this test, we could conclude that the mean number of questions answered differs at the 0.05 level of significance, with a p-value < 0.001. Therefore, for Group 123, with a 95% confidence level, we can reject (5)________ *"H_{0A}—The use of the proposed methodology does not allow users to cover more analytical questions"*.

In order to accept or reject the null hypothesis *"H_{0B}: The use of the proposed methodology does not improve the set of generated visualizations"*, the answers of the rubric have been analyzed. The participants scored the visualizations created without methodology with an average 1.82/4. (6)________, the visualizations generated using the methodology presented were scored with an average of 2.74/4.

The 2-Sample T-Test was performed with an alpha of 0.05. Thanks to this test, we could conclude that for Group 123, with a 95% confidence level, we can reject the null hypothesis H_{0B}.

- Group 4: 39 college computer engineering students from UCLM who were not given assistance in carrying out the experiment.

In accordance with the results obtained, the set of visualizations generated without following any methodology can answer 2.13/4 (53%) of the specific questions proposed, while this number grows until 2.34/4 (59%) when following the proposed method. However, in this case, the 2-Sample T-Test concludes that with a *p*-value of 0.430, the number of questions answered is not significantly different. Therefore, for "Group 4", we cannot reject the null hypothesis H_{0A}.

Consistent with the results of Group 123, H_{0B} was rejected with the 2-Sample T-Test was performed with an alpha of 0.05.

- Group 5: 13 employees of a small IT company who were assisted while carrying out the experiment.

The results of Group 5 presents similar trends with Group 123. Both H_{0A} and H_{0B} were rejected after the 2-Sample T-Test.

Finally, as in the previous cases, Fig. 14 reflects the normality of the data, as well as the difference of the averages. Therefore, the normality of our data is confirmed.

In conclusion, the T-test results showed statistical significance for the results obtained, confirming the impact of the methodology proposed. Fig. 15 summarizes the score given to the improvement of one method over the other through the third question of rubric. In most cases the participants have (7)________ when using our methodology.

4.2 Analysis of Visualizations

Through comparing the visualizations generated freely and those generated using our methodology, it could be found that, by following our methodology, a larger number of visualizations were created than by creating them freely. (8)________ 205 visualizations were created freely (an average of 2.11 per participant), while 257 visualizations were created by following our methodology (an average of 2.65 per participant).

Moreover, we have analyzed the types of visualizations selected in each case. When the participants did the exercise freely, the most used visualization types were Column Graph, Pie Chart, and Map. Nevertheless, when the participants did the exercise following our methodology, the most used visualizations were Column Graph, Map, and Bubble Graph.

4.3 Discussion

The experiments increase our confidence about the utility of our methodology. It significantly improves over the case when users face the same problem manually. (9)________: (i) users are allowed to cover more analytical questions, (ii) the visualizations produced are more effective, and (iii) the overall satisfaction of the users is larger.

5. Conclusion: By following our proposal, non-expert users will be able to more effectively express their analytical needs and obtain the set of visualizations that best suits their goals.

(Adapted from "A methodology to automatically translate user requirements into visualizations: Experimental validation" by Lavalle, A., Maté, A., Trujillo, J., Teruel, A. M. & Rizzi, S. in *Information and Software Technology,* Vol. 136, 2021.)

1. Read the article and fill in the blanks with the following words or expressions. Change the form if necessary.

A. cover

B. specifically

C. grouped

D. a total of

E. with reference to

F. underlying problems

G. the null hypothesis

H. comparatively

I. detect an improvement

2. Read the following descriptions about results and discussion. Judge whether the statements are true or false.

	Descriptions about results and discussion	True	False
1	The results and discussion section creates a natural transition from how the study was designed to what the study reveals.		
2	It is unexpected to have tables and graphics, where relevant, to contextualize and illustrate the data.		
3	The results chapter should provide a direct and factual account of the data collected without any interpretation of the findings.		
4	The discussion answers the research questions and responds to any hypotheses proposed.		
5	Unexpected or contradictory data can be ignored and not explained.		
6	When discussing the results, it is important to compare the findings with those of other researchers.		
7	Whilst the results chapter is strictly factual, reporting on the data on a surface level, the discussion is rooted in analysis and interpretation.		
8	Although there may be some repetition of information in results and discussion, it should be kept without any deduction.		
9	The discussion moves from specific results to general implications.		
10	It is not advised to include the limitations of the study and follow up with some recommendations for future research.		

Project

Work in groups. You need to:

1. Collect the results and discussion section of 5 top journal articles and 5 MA theses written by Chinese students in English.
2. Evaluate the results and discussion section of these 10 articles/theses according to the checklist below.
3. Compare them and discuss how to improve the results and discussion section of the MA theses.

4. Discuss with your group members and prepare a report for presentation in class.

Checklist of well-written results and discussion				
Items		Yes	No	Not necessary
1	**Content**			
	Overall description of the experiments			
	Representative data			
	Interpretation of results			
	Major findings			
	Comparison with previous research			
	Exceptions			
	Limitations			
	Implications or applications			
	Unanswered questions for future research			
2	**Wording/Style**			
	Past tense			
	Academic expressions			
	Objective			
	Clarity			
	Internal consistency with the remaining parts			

Unit 7

Conclusions

Part I
Introducing the Unit

A good conclusion in a research paper, by bringing a close to the argument presented and proposing future research directions, leaves the readers with a strong impression. To make the paper well-knit in structure, the conclusion should be coherent with the title, introduction and discussion. It aims both to "look back" and to "look forward". By "looking back", it restates the main argument and findings and points out limitations to the research. By "looking forward", it gives suggestions for improvement on the limitations and speculates on unexplored fields.

In this unit, we are going to read and analyze some samples from journal articles to better understand the content and functions of the conclusion of research papers.

Part II
Reading for Expressions

Study the bold-faced expressions that are often used in the conclusion section of a research paper.

Restating the Research Aim

- **The objective of this review was to summarize** the current best evidence for the effectiveness of VR interventions for the rehabilitation of people with Parkinson's Disease.
- **The purpose of the current study was to determine** the effect of illustrations on bridging inferences, an important aspect of meaning making in comprehension models.
- **This study set out to attempt to investigate** the causes of this heterogeneity **and so identify** factors associated with good health gains.
- **This paper has argued that** a mixture of procedures is required for the evaluation of a macroeconomic model.
- **A** concept level **study was undertaken to** design and analyze a possible aircraft configuration.

Presenting Results/Findings

- **It was found that** ERBB2 was overexpressed in about 25% of the gastric primary tumor models, which correlates with the higher level of CD90 expression in these tumors.
- **It can be concluded that** the preparation of homogeneous mixtures with arbitrary composition from a pair of compatible polymers and a common solvent is only possible on rare occasions.
- **These data demonstrate that** an aged, senescent immune system has a causal role in driving systemic ageing and therefore represents a key therapeutic target to extend healthy ageing.
- **The results of this investigation show that** there is a good agreement between experimental and predicted values indicating desirable validity of the model.

- **The results of this study indicate that** the solar wind interaction with the bow shock is far more dynamic than previously imagined and far more significant to the solar wind-magnetosphere interaction.
- **Taken together, these results suggest that** inhibition of COX-2 is one of the mechanisms by which the methanolic extract of adlay seed inhibits cancer growth and prevents lung tumorigenesis.
- **The results highlight the importance of** both the stabilization mechanism and capping agent chemistry as key factors governing the transport of AgNPs in the environment.

Conveying Implications

- **The findings** reported here **shed new light on** the flexibility of combinatorial control mechanisms in endomesoderm specification in Caenorhabditis.
- **Our results open a new approach for** BCIs and demonstrate the feasibility of accurately decoding rapid, dexterous movements years after paralysis.
- **This study contributes to** our understanding of the role of pets in the daily management of long-term mental health problems.
- **This study lays the groundwork for** future molecular studies of Apis neuropeptides with the identification of 36 genes, 33 of which were previously unreported.

Presenting Limitations

- **A major limitation of the study was** our inability to segregate thrombotic from hemorrhagic strokes.
- **This study was limited by** uncertainty of the diagnosis of asthma as it was only a physician's diagnosis without chest radiography or lung function tests.

Making Recommendations

- **Further research is required to determine** whether physiological changes simply result from the neurodegeneration process or also modify the neurodegenerative process, thereby providing a novel therapeutic target.
- **Further research should focus on** understanding carbohydrate metabolism in cats and establishing an equation that accurately predicts the metabolizable energy of feline diets.

Part III Reading for Ideas

Passage A

Pre-reading tasks:

1. What are the steps involved in writing the conclusion of a research paper?
2. In what ways does the conclusion differ from the abstract?

The Function of the Conclusion Section

The function of the paper's conclusion is to restate the main argument. It reminds the reader of the strengths of the argument: That is, it reiterates the most important evidence supporting the argument. Make sure, however, that your conclusion is not simply a repetitive summary as this reduces the impact of the argument you have developed in your paper. Given that the reader has now been presented with all the information about the topic, the conclusion provides a forum for you to persuasively and succinctly restate your thesis. Depending on the discipline you are writing in, the concluding paragraph may also contain a reflection on the evidence presented, or on the paper's thesis. The nature of the reflection will depend on your topic (Woodward-Kron, 1997), but questions such as these may be considered:

- What is the significance of your findings?
- What are the implications of your conclusions for this topic and for the broader field?
- Are there any limitations to your approach?
- Are there any other factors of relevance that impact upon the topic, but fell outside the scope of the paper?
- Are there any suggestions you can make in terms of future research?

The conclusion should match the introduction in terms of the ideas presented and the argument put forward. Sometimes you will find that the process of writing has changed what you have argued and so it will be necessary to go back and reword the introduction. Finally, the conclusion is not the place in your paper to introduce new information or new ideas: These should be in the body of your paper.

(Retrieved from University of Wollongong Australia website.)

Fill in the blanks:

The abstract usually gives the readers the first impression of the paper, while the conclusion is the very last part of the research paper, allowing the readers to better understand why the paper should matter to them. The conclusion needs to restate the (1) _______ of the research, summarize main research (2) _______, suggest (3) _______ for the field of knowledge, explain the (4) _______ of the findings or contribution of the research, recognize the (5) _______ of the current research, and make (6) _______ for the future research work.

Passage B

Pre-reading tasks:

1. What are the elements of a good conclusion?
2. How can the conclusion be linked with the introduction to tie the research paper together?

How to Develop a Conclusion

A well-written conclusion provides you with several important opportunities to demonstrate your overall understanding of the research problem to the reader. These include:

- **Presenting the last word on the issues you raised in your paper.** Just as the introduction gives a first impression to your reader, the conclusion offers a chance to leave a lasting impression. Do this, for example, by highlighting key points in your analysis or findings.
- **Summarizing your thoughts and conveying the larger implications of your study.** The conclusion is an opportunity to succinctly answer the "so what?"

question by placing the study within the context of past research about the topic you've investigated.

- **Demonstrating the importance of your ideas.** Don't be shy. The conclusion offers you a chance to elaborate on the significance of your findings.
- **Introducing possible new or expanded ways of thinking about the research problem.** This does not refer to introducing new information (which should be avoided), but to offer new insight and creative approaches for framing/contextualizing the research problem based on the results of your study.

There are several problems to avoid in developing a conclusion. These include:

- **Failure to be concise**

The conclusion section should be concise and to the point. Conclusions that are too long often have unnecessary details. The conclusion section is not the place for details about your methodology or results. Although you should give a summary of what was learned from your research, this summary should be relatively brief, since the emphasis in the conclusion is on the implications, evaluations, insights, etc. that you make.

- **Failure to comment on larger, more significant issues**

In the introduction, your task was to move from general (the field of study) to specific (your research problem). However, in the conclusion, your task is to move from specific (your research problem) back to general (your field, i.e., how your research contributes new understanding or fills an important gap in the literature). In other words, the conclusion is where you place your research within a larger context.

- **Failure to reveal problems and negative results**

Negative aspects of the research process should never be ignored. Problems, drawbacks, and challenges encountered during your study should be included as a way of qualifying your overall conclusions. If you encountered negative results (findings that are validated outside the research context in which they were generated), you must report them in the results section of your paper. In the conclusion, use the negative results as an opportunity to explain how they provide information on which future research can be based.

- **Failure to provide a clear summary of what was learned**

In order to be able to discuss how your research fits back into your field of study (and possibly the world at large), you need to summarize it briefly and directly. Often this element of your conclusion is only a few sentences long.

- **Failure to match the objectives of your research**

Often research objectives change while the research is being carried out. This is not a problem unless you forget to go back and refine your original objectives in your introduction, as these changes emerge, they must be documented so that they accurately reflect what you were trying to accomplish in your research (not what you thought you might accomplish when you began).

(Retrieved from Sacred Heart University Library website.)

Fill in the blanks:

A good conclusion needs to be concise and engaging, leaving the readers with a strong impression. It (1) ________ the introduction in the research paper by bringing better closure to what the introduction announces. It does not introduce (2) ________ findings or arguments; instead, it helps the readers to refocus on the most important points in the (3) ________, indicate important (4) ________ and relevant (5) ________ of the research.

Part IV
Reading for Speaking

Read the conclusions in the following two passages, and then discuss the questions in groups.

Passage A

Emerging and Evolving Concepts in Gene Essentiality

Conclusion

In conclusion, recent technological advances have enabled massive genome-wide screening efforts that are uncovering the complex and multifaceted nature of essential genes. From the several examples herein reviewed, it is evident that gene essentiality is not a fixed property of a gene, but strongly depends on the environmental and genetic context, and can be altered in the course of both short-term and long-term evolution. Thus, the essentiality of a gene is a quantitative rather than a binary trait, and should be measured on a continuous scale. This idea could be further extended by claiming that no gene is absolutely essential—only functions can be so. These emerging concepts are opening up exciting avenues for fundamental research into the basic requirements for life, as well as illuminating new paths towards therapeutic exploitation against diseases, spanning from cancer to infectious diseases.

Some of the key next steps include re-assessing gene essentiality in the light of its context-dependent and quantitative nature; not only in the few model organisms, but also in non-model organisms across the tree of life. This assessment will be instrumental not only for understanding the evolutionary plasticity of essential cellular functions, but also for gaining more knowledge of medically and industrially relevant microorganisms. Once systematic quantifications of gene essentiality are available for a large number of species, the next leap will be to understand how these genes are interconnected within the cell. GI maps need to become truly "genome-wide" and not only focus on non-essential genes, which could be accomplished by employing hypomorphic, temperature-sensitive or repressible alleles of essential genes. By comprehensively mapping connections within and between cellular pathways across various species and environmental conditions, these studies will facilitate our understanding of archetypal network design principles, higher-level organization of vital processes and principles underlying drug resistance. Comprehensive gene–gene and gene–drug interaction maps can also be used as a basis for machine learning approaches to predict the outcome of combination therapies. Although drug combinations are often the preferred strategy for treating many diseases, there is currently limited knowledge for the rational design of combination therapies and for predicting their efficacy, mode of action and the likelihood of emergence of resistance. A comprehensive understanding of the identity of, and interconnection between essential cellular processes represents an ideal platform on which to build such predictive models.

(Adapted from "Emerging and evolving concepts in gene essentiality" by Rancati G. et al. in *Nat Rev Genet*, Vol. 19, 2018.)

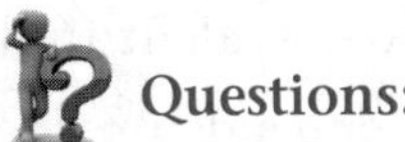

Questions:

1. This is a review on a founding concept of genetics and gene essentiality. What do Paragraph 1 and Paragraph 2 talk about respectively?
2. What should be emphasized in the conclusion of this passage?
3. How could you introduce new insight instead of new information when writing a conclusion?

Passage B

Multi-Scale Analyses on the Ecosystem Services in the Chinese Loess Plateau and Implications for Dryland Sustainability

Conclusion

With the promotion of the 2030 sustainable development goals, ecological restoration will be increasingly used as a powerful tool for realizing the target of land degradation neutrality. This is particularly important and challenging in global drylands. The ecosystem service research has provided scientific support for quantifying the effectiveness and impacts of ecological restoration on drylands just as those reflected from the research progresses reviewed in this paper on the Chinese Loess Plateau region. To further advance the ecosystem service science in a systematic socio-ecological perspective, the research needs to be directed towards multidisciplinary and transdisciplinary approaches to uncover the mechanisms on the production and flow of ecosystem services, and their contributions to human well-being and socioeconomic development in global drylands. Dryland sustainability can also be facilitated by science informed dryland management that promotes restoration and mitigates degradation by harmonizing human-nature relations from local to global scales.

(Adapted from "Multi-scale analyses on the ecosystem services in the Chinese Loess Plateau and implications for dryland sustainability" by Lv Y. H. et al. in *Current Opinion in Environmental Sustainability*, Vol. 48, 2021.)

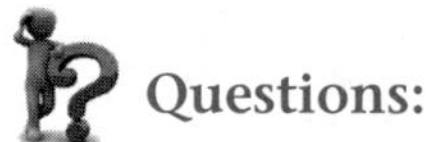

1. How is this conclusion organized?
2. What are the implications in the conclusion of this research?
3. How does the author look at the issue of dryland management?

Part V
Reading for Writing

A conclusion summarizes the findings and proposes new directions of the research. Read Passage A and Passage B in "Reading for Speaking" and write a summary with no less than 200 words that answers the following questions:

- What are the main purposes of the conclusion part of a research paper?
- What elements does a conclusion contain?
- What general rules should you follow when writing a conclusion?

Exercises

I. Improve the following conclusion in terms of wording, style and structure.

In conclusion, our study illustrates the liver immune profiling of pathogenesis of BA. We found that CX3CR1$^+$ CD8Teff cells inhibited fibrosis, demonstrated that the deficiency of CX3CR1-expressing T cells contribute to liver fibrosis in BA. We discovered the B cell lymphopoiesis did not cease after birth and that tolerance defects contributed to IgG accumulation in BA. Furthermore, B-cell-modifying therapies could ameliorate liver pathology in the RRV-induced BA mouse model. Further studies focusing on therapeutics are required to fully validate these findings.

II. Read the following conclusion, and then do the exercises.

Conclusion

Here, we have ***highlighted*** the unique features of hydrogel-based soft robots and ***described*** their potential applications as well as their fundamental working mechanisms. The past decade has ***brought an explosion of*** hydrogel-based ***applications to*** the field of soft robotics. The unique properties of hydrogels have allowed them to play outstanding roles and endow soft robots with innovative functionalities. Even though recent efforts have ***proved the feasibility*** of hydrogels as a material for soft robots, the field is still in its early stages and such robots are far from use in daily life. ***Approaches*** beyond the proof-of-concept level pose several issues that ***need to be explored***. Here, we ***suggest*** future directions for hydrogel-based soft robotics in three realms:

With the recent increased interest in versatile soft robots, a tremendous amount of effort has been ***focused on*** hydrogels because most of them can respond to diverse stimuli, such as solvents, temperature, humidity, and so on. Multi stimuli-responsiveness is an attractive feature that extends the range of applications of hydrogels in the field of soft robotics. However, it ***raises a new issue*** originating from stimulus interference. To secure reliability, a hydrogel must be capable of distinguishing between a desirable stimulus and undesirable stimuli in accordance with a given situation. This remains an unaddressed challenge and ***open area of***

exploration. The introduction of stimuli-selectivity will ***spur*** significant developments in hydrogel-based soft robotics by securing reliable controllability.

Although there have been explosive efforts that have enhanced the mechanical and electrical properties of hydrogels, the challenge of durability has rarely been met. First, dehydration of the hydrogel is a critical issue in open-air environments because evaporation deteriorates the properties of a hydrogel, including softness, transparency, and ionic conductivity. Recently, several attempts have been made to ***address this challenge***. For instance, introducing humectants such as hygroscopic salts is a simple strategy to reduce the vapor pressure of water. However, it is not ideal because hydrogels containing humectants can undesirably swell in humid conditions. Using an elastomeric coating as a diffusion barrier against water is another noteworthy strategy. However, this approach has trade-offs because it deteriorates some fascinating features of the material, such as biocompatibility, stretchability, transparency, etc. Second, electrochemical stability is a crucial issue because electrochemical reactions inevitably occur at the interface between a hydrogel and an electronic conductor when the applied voltage exceeds the electrochemical window. This causes undesirable side reactions and reduces the concentration of the ionic charge carrier. While there have been valuable attempts to use hydrogels under high-voltage conditions, their utility remains limited to capacitive operating systems or AC voltage applications. Addressing the elusive challenges mentioned above without sacrificing the fascinating properties of hydrogels will help to provide further enhancements.

With the advent of hydrogel-based soft robotics, researchers have ***proven the potential of*** hydrogel-based robotic components, including actuators, sensors, communicators, power sources, and computational circuits. While the individual components have been tremendously well-researched, the effort to combine individual components into a single system remains in its infancy. Systemization of the well-established individual components is an essential ***prerequisite for*** real-world application of hydrogel-based soft robotics. Beyond simple physical combining, complementary interactions between all components promise to fulfill the maximum potential of soft robotics—the ability to operate without further intervention. At the same time, the systemization process should not deteriorate the compliancy of the soft robots; care must be taken to preserve their unique features. Fundamental insights into the underlying working principle of each individual component gleaned from a multidisciplinary approach may help to address daunting challenges and ***open new avenues*** for further innovation in the field of soft robotics.

(Adapted from "Hydrogel soft robotics" by Lee Y. et al. in *Materials Today Physics*, Vol. 15, 2020.)

1. **Fill in the blanks with the italicized words or expressions from the text above. Change the form if necessary.**

   1) Three possible ________ of research suggested themselves.

   2) Our curiosity leads us to ________ the challenge of establishing robust and secure communication channels.

   3) A command of information is the necessary ________ to the scientific consideration of any subject.

   4) This session will ________ technology trends in distribution management from analytics to gamification.

   5) They ________ all their attention on finding a solution to the problem.

   6) The asteroid retrieval mission for 2021 aims to prove the ________ of capturing and relocating an asteroid.

2. **Answer the following questions according to the text above.**

   1) What elements are involved in this conclusion?

   2) What could be the possible subheadings for Paragraphs 2, 3 and 4?

   3) A conclusion is an overview of what you have done in conducting your research. From what perspective should you write a conclusion?

3. **Read the conclusion above, and then rearrange the following sentences into a well-organized abstract by numbering them from 1 to 7.**

   ________ Furthermore, hydrogels provide innovative capabilities for soft robotics based on their unique responsiveness to stimuli.

_______ To boost progress in the field, there is a need for compliant materials.

_______ With the rapidly growing attention to human-robot interfaces, soft robotics has attracted a great deal of interest.

_______ Finally, we suggest perspectives on future directions that addressing potential challenges in the field of hydrogel soft robotics.

_______ Hydrogels are promising as compliant materials for soft robots because of their outstanding features, including high stretchability, transparency, ionic conductivity, and biocompatibility.

_______ In this review, we discuss the unique features of hydrogel-based soft robots, from their fundamental working mechanisms to notable applications.

_______ Soft robots have diverse advantages, including compliancy and safety, which contribute to seamless interactions with humans.

III. Read the following abridged research paper, and write a paragraph of no less than 150 words to discuss the relationship between the conclusion part and the rest of the paper.

1. Introduction

The fifth generation (5G) systems will enable people to access and share information in a wide range of scenarios with extremely low latency and very high data rate. It should achieve 1,000 times the system capacity, 100 times the data rate, 3–5 times the spectral efficiency, and 10–100 times the energy efficiency with respect to the current fourth generation (4G) systems. To the best of the authors' knowledge, a survey paper for 5G channel measurements and models covering various 5G technologies/scenarios and presenting the latest channel models of different standardization organizations is still missing. This paper aims to fill this gap. The major contributions of this paper are summarized as follows:

(1) The requirements for 5G channel modeling are highlighted. The most important channel measurements are reviewed in terms of different scenarios (applications and frequency bands). New propagation characteristics are introduced and their underlying propagation mechanisms are discussed.

(2) The scenario-specific 5G channel models are presented. For each scenario, the state-of-the-art modeling approaches are introduced and compared in a comprehensive manner.

(3) General 5G channel models covering more scenarios and proposed by different organizations are presented. The pros and cons of each general model are discussed. A comprehensive comparison of those models is proposed.

(4) Future research directions for 5G and beyond 5G (B5G) channel measurements and modeling are outlined.

The rest of this paper is organized as follows. In Section II, an overview of 5G channel measurements and propagation properties is presented. Existing 5G channel models for various scenarios are provided in Section III. General 5G channel models covering more scenarios are introduced in Section IV. Future research directions for 5G and B5G channel measurements and models are outlined in Section V. Finally, conclusions are drawn in Section VI.

2. 5G Channel Measurements

In this section, we will briefly review several representative channel measurements in the light of different 5G communication technologies. New propagation properties caused by 5G communication technologies in different propagation environments were reported in the following measurement campaigns and should be considered carefully in 5G channel modeling.

3. Scenario-Specific 5G Channel Models

According to the modeling approach, channel models can be classified into stochastic channel models and deterministic channel models. Stochastic channel models describe channel parameters using certain probability distributions. Generally speaking, stochastic channel models are mathematically tractable and can be adapted to various scenarios with relatively low accuracy (compared with deterministic channel models). Deterministic channel models predict the propagation waves in a more accurate manner by solving the Maxwells equations or approximated propagation equations. Deterministic channel models usually introduce high computational complexity and rely on precise information of the propagation environments. More detailed classification of 5G channel models and their definitions can be found in Fig. 2 and Table II, respectively. In this section, 5G channel models in the literature are reviewed and classified in terms of different communication technologies or scenarios. These technologies introduce distinctly different propagation characteristics compared to those of conventional channels and pose new challenges to the 5G channel modeling. We will briefly introduce these challenges and review the approaches to overcome them.

4. General 5G Channel Models

In this section, we will introduce ten up-to-date general 5G channel models, which are COST 2100 channel model, MiWEBA channel model, QuaDRiGa, mmMAGIC channel model, METIS channel model, 5GCMSIG, 3GPP channel model, IMT-2020 channel model, IEEE 802.11ay, and more general 5G channel models (MG5GCM). The "general" means the channel models can support various 5G communication technologies and can be adapted to different scenarios. All of these channel models, except MiWEBA and IEEE 802.11ay channel models, can be classified as GBSMs or adopted GBSMs since their primary modules root from SCM and WINNER II channel models. The grid-based GBSM (GGBSM) was first presented by METIS and then adopted by 5GCMSIG and mmMAGIC. It was developed in order to provide a smooth time evolution and spatially consistent simulations through interpolating channel parameters among the nearest grids in a 2D map. The deterministic modeling approach, i.e., map-based approach, proposed by METIS, was developed based on a simple 3D geometrical environment to provide an accurate and realistic channel data. The map-based hybrid model was first proposed by METIS and 3GPP, and then admitted by IMT-2020. It was developed by combining a GBSM and a map-based model. The map-based hybrid model can provide a flexible and scalable simulation, and at the same time can achieve a trade-off between accuracy and complexity. Besides a GBSM and a map-based hybrid model, the IMT-2020 also proposed an extension module based on the time-spatial propagation (TSP) model. It was used as an alternative modeling method to generate channel parameters by taking into account environment-specific parameters such as street width, building height, etc. Considering the quasi-optical characteristics of mmWave bands, the MiWEBA and IEEE 802.11ay proposed a quasi-deterministic (Q-

D) modeling approach by combining the deterministic approach and the stochastic approach. The Q-D approach was reported to have the ability to meet the major challenges of outdoor channel modeling at 60 GHz.

5. Future Research Directions for 5G and B5G Channel Measurements and Models

Apart from the above-mentioned topics, there are still many debates over the specifications of future channel measurements and models. Most future researches will focus on developing channel models which are more efficient (combining multiple modeling approaches), covering extremely wide frequency bands (e.g., terahertz (THz) spectrum and visible light spectrum), concentrating on new scenarios (e.g., tunnel, underground, underwater, and even the human body), and combining with other disciplines (e.g., big data and machine learning).

6. Conclusions

This paper has provided a comprehensive review of key topics in 5G channel measurements and modeling. Requirements for the 5G channel modeling have been provided. Existing channel measurements and models for the most challenging communication scenarios in 5G systems, i.e., massive MIMO communication, V2V communication, HST communication, and mmWave communication, have been reviewed and discussed. General channel models covering more 5G scenarios have been introduced and a comparison of these models has been provided. Future research directions for 5G and B5G channel measurements and models have been outlined. The 5G channel models should simulate wireless propagation channels over an extremely wide frequency range, covering various network topologies, and can be adapted to a great number of scenarios. In the future, multiple channel modeling approaches or hybrid channel modeling approaches rather than one modeling approach may be adopted, in order to address all the challenges caused by 5G systems and at the same time, achieve a good trade-off between model accuracy and complexity.

(Adapted from "A survey of 5G channel measurements and models" by Wang C. X. et al. in *IEEE Communications Surveys & Tutorials*, Vol. 99, 2018.)

Project

Work in groups. Collect the conclusions of 10 research papers of your interest after class. You need to:

1. Identify what elements are included in all the papers.
2. Identify the words and expressions that are most frequently used to summarize the findings and propose future directions in the papers.
3. Prepare a report for presentation in class.

Checklist of a well-written conclusion		
Content	Yes	No
Restatement of the aims		
Main findings		
Implications		
Limitations		
Recommendations		

Unit 8

Reviewers' Comments

Part I
Introducing the Unit

Journals generally depend on peer review to ensure the quality of the papers they publish. Reviewers' comments are a kind of feedback given by peer professionals after they examine the papers. In the comments, the reviewers usually point out problems in the paper and give some suggestions for submitting authors to improve their work. Their comments also help the editors to decide what to publish. Thus, understanding reviewers' comments facilitates researchers to produce publishable papers.

In this unit, we will read about the criteria and requirements followed in peer review by analyzing several examples of comments from reviewers in terms of how to write an excellent paper for the purpose of academic research and publication.

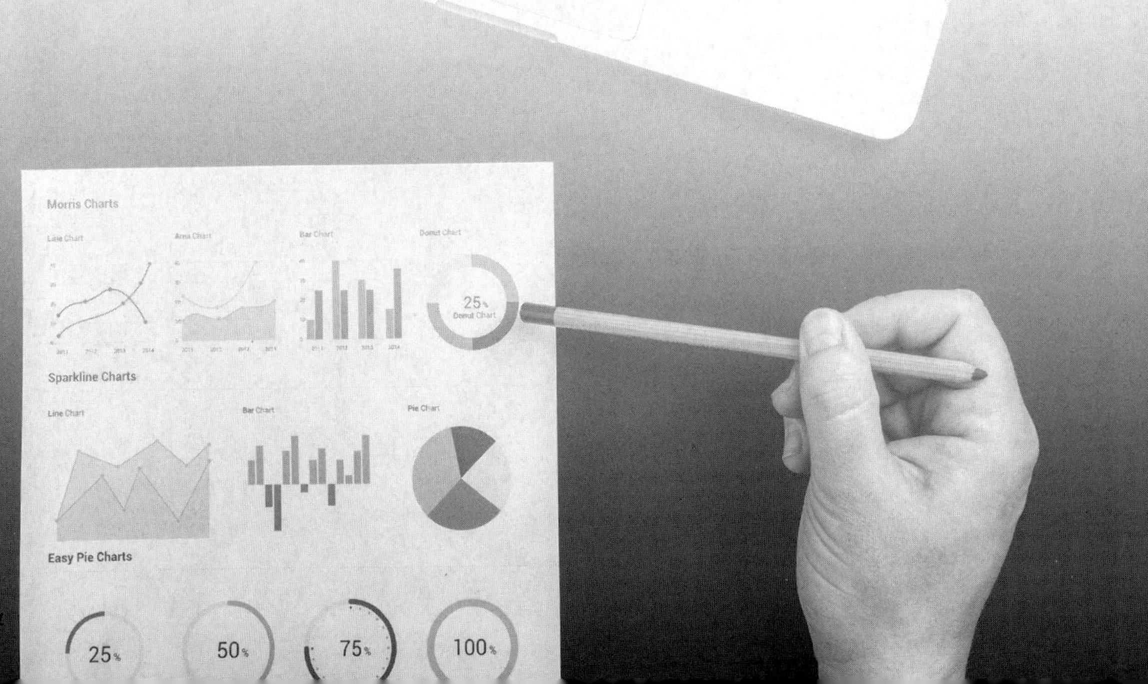

Part II
Reading for Expressions

Study the bold-faced expressions that are often used in the reviewers' comments on a paper.

General Comments to Editors

- I think the paper could be **acceptable for publication** as it is, but I do have a few comments that might **improve the presentation** to a broader audience.
- If the authors could **address these major concerns**, then I would support publication in *Nature*.
- **Given these restrictions**, I leave it to the editor to decide whether this study should be published in *Nature* or another journal such as...

About Introduction and Literature Review

- This paper **lacks** a detailed literature review on the renewable potentials, current profile, relevant research methods, which are referred to for this study.
- **Due to** the topic of the work I **highly recommend** the authors to have a look at G and S: S M, 2003/04 (a reference), who have presented some very similar ideas in their work.

About Research Methods

- The authors should present a scientific procedure with the methodology **explained in detail**.
- However, the reason why I've given this paper a Neutral recommendation is because it seems to **overlook** the "why" and **focus too much on** the "what".
- So, more details about **the true potential and/or limitation** of the presented approach beyond human would make this study more attractive for a broader audience.

About Results and Discussion

- We should have a lot of such papers that **give honest views** of results, and that **extend** their evaluations to check for other anomalies.
- The key points (whatever the authors determine to be key) should be **clear** in abstract, results, and then discussed, explained, and their significance **explained** in the discussion.
- In my opinion, the results are **too descriptive** and **lack technical discussion**, even if a very brief one.

About Data and Graphics

- The study is well written and **illustrated with intuitive figures**.
- The section "Mix of generation capacities and power generation" presents some **arbitrary data** and information **without scientific reasoning and process**.
- Error bars are missing and **so it is not completely evident if** the difference is significant.

About Wording and Style

- The language **is poor with** grammar issues and typos.
- The sentence wording here is **not abundantly clear** on why the ONT reads harbor more sequence variation.
- The writing style is **far away from** scientific writing, e.g., what is the supporting information, such as data or reference, for the following statement?

About Innovativeness

- This research direction is **promising**, but **more effort** needs to go into this project.
- The authors have **put forth** significant effort and the apparent intent of this report could be **of great value**.
- It allows to **advance** in the so-called "giant planet energy crisis", **presenting new insight on** the ionosphere-magnetosphere coupling at Jupiter.

Part III
Reading for Ideas

Passage A

Pre-reading task:

1. What are to be reviewed by experts and editors in peer review?
2. As a first-time-author, what is the primary consideration before writing?

Suggestions for Reviewers and Authors

Criteria for Reviewers to Evaluate Manuscripts

(1) Do the research and the results present a significant new advance to a clearly identified technological problem or scientific question?

(2) Are the objectives of the research clearly defined, and is the research in line with the objectives?

(3) Is the introduction clearly presented, and confined to the research objective?

(4) Are the experimental methods appropriate, and are they described clearly and with sufficient details for the work to be repeatable?

(5) Are the data quantitative, understandable, and presented clearly?

(6) Is the statistical treatment of the data adequate?

(7) Are the results and conclusions clearly presented and do they support the claims made by the authors?

(8) Is the discussion integrated with the results, clearly presented and confined to the research data?

(9) Are the language, grammar, and style of high standard?

(10) Are the figures and tables of high quality?

(11) Does the title adequately reflect the content of the manuscript?

(12) Can the abstract be understood on its own and does it contain the relevant facts?

(13) Are the most relevant references all cited, can unnecessary or marginally relevant references be omitted?

What Readers and Editors Want

If you are a first-time author. you need to consider what it might take to get journal readers interested in a paper. Before you start to write, have your target readers in mind. Start by thinking clearly who will be primary and secondary readers of the work and how they might benefit from learning about your work. Consider the following questions:

(1) Who are likely to be the main readers of a paper on this work?

(2) Who else might read the paper?

(3) What is likely to be the background of the main readers and other potential readers? What are the readers' jobs?

(4) What will interest the readers in the paper? What is the main point of interest to the likely readers?

(5) How much experience are the readers likely to have with the subject?

(6) Are the readers likely to be familiar with the situation or circumstances being described in the paper?

(7) Why do the readers need to read the paper? From the author's point of view, what is to be learned from the paper?

(8) What do you want readers to do after reading the paper?

Most readers will want details about an author's work. They will want to know why you carried out the work, an overview of the previous research on the subject, the approach and methods used, the findings and their interpretation and the conclusions. An editor wants everything that readers want and more. An editor wants to publish papers that interest and excite the journal's readers, that are important to advancing knowledge in the field and that spark new ideas for work in the field. An editor also wants papers that are consistent with both the journal's aims and Instructions for Authors and that are well written. Finally, an editor wants to publish papers that give a true and accurate picture of the work undertaken.

(Adapted from《SCI 论文写作和发表：You Can Do It》by Zhang, J. D. & Yang, Q. Z., 2016; "Writing for publication—a guide for new authors" by Dixon, N. in *International Journal for Quality in Health Care*, Vol. 13, 2001.)

 **Fill in the blanks:**

Being aware of the criteria of peer review renders you to publish your own essay. The criteria require the (1) ________ to be confined to the research objective, experimental methods to contain sufficient details and be (2) ________, and discussion to be integrated with (3) ________. In scientific papers, experiments are the key part. Whether the data are (4) ________, understandable and presented clearly is also under reviewer' consideration. Thus, the (5) ________ that present the data must be of high quality. As a first-time-author, writing a paper might be arduous. Considering your (6) ________ readers and trying to make your paper cater for their main point of (7) ________ and scope of understanding. Then the readers can (8) ________ from the paper as much as possible.

Passage B

 **Pre-reading tasks:**

1. What should be paid special attention to in data presentation?
2. What should be presented in the discussion section?

Requirements for Reviewers to Evaluate Manuscripts

Regarding the **Introduction**, here are some practical rules including: (1) to expose the nature of the problem with insight, in order to catch the reader's attention; (2) to check carefully the relevant bibliography, with the purpose of guiding the reader; (3) to select the method, in such a way that the reader understands what the problem was and how it was solved; (4) to mention the principal results of the survey; (5) to define the principal conclusions suggested by the results. The reader must not be kept in suspense as regards the obtained results.

In the chapter dealing with **Materials and Methods**, it has a critical importance because the cornerstone of the scientific method requires that the results be reproducible. A good referee should pay special attention to this section of the text; in case of doubt regarding the possibility of reproducing the experiments, he/she should reject the paper, even if the results and conclusions are outstanding.

In the chapter on **Results**, the text should be short and objective without verbosity. The data need to be presented simply and clearly, since they represent new knowledge emerging in the world. The tendency to repeat results in words should be avoided.

Regarding the **Discussion**, avoiding redundancy is of great importance and in this section, the paper results are to be explained and commented upon, but never summed up. Scientists must be levelheaded, but not shy, exposing with lucidity and courage the theoretical consequences and the possible practical applications of their researches.

(Adapted from "Book review: How to write and publish scientific papers" by Day, R. A. in *Memórias do Instituto Oswaldo Cruz*, Vol. 93, No. 3, 1998.)

Fill in the blanks:

Results and discussion can sometimes be confusing since the boundary between them is not so clear to some submitting authors. In results chapter, data should be displayed simply and (1) _______. (2) _______ results ought to be avoided since the research data represent (3) _______ knowledge emerging in the world. In discussion part, (4) _______ and comments are needed, but (5) _______ should be excluded. Meanwhile, theoretical (6) _______ and possible practical (7) _______ of the researches can be pointed out in (8) _______.

Part IV
Reading for Speaking

Read the following peer reviews, and then discuss the questions in groups.

Passage A

Referee #1 (Remarks to the Author):

The paper "Global heating of Jupiter's upper atmosphere by auroral energy circulation" by O'Donoghue and colleagues presents new measurements of the Jovian atmosphere obtained with NIRSPEC at the Keck II telescope in April 2016 and January 2017. Auroral emissions are investigated to derive $H3^+$ ion concentration and temperature through intensity ratio of $H3^+$ lines. An increased temperature is observed in case of the reported measurements in January 2017 that is explained with an excess of auroral energy distributed in the upper atmosphere.

The study proposed in the manuscript is new and interesting for the astronomical community. It allows to advance in the so-called "giant planet energy crisis", presenting new insight on the ionosphere-magnetosphere coupling at Jupiter. The paper is well written and clearly explains the observations and analysis. The paper is suitable for publication on the Journal. However, there are few points that are missing in my opinion:

A comparison with other measurements, for example with the Juno observations in a period close to the ones reported in the paper, would be helpful in getting a wider picture of the Jovian atmosphere. For example, Juno measurements during the 4th passage on 1st February 2017 would be useful to check if a similar temperature enhancement is still present few days after the data obtained by the authors.

I would also suggest to discuss the JTGCM model results (Bougher et al., 2005, JGR 110, doi:10.1029/2003JE002230) and compare the observed features to this model. It shows that the observed Jovian temperatures and densities in the thermosphere can be satisfactorily matched with a combination of auroral particle and Joule heating at low and high latitudes.

Sentence at line 111 is confusing: Temperatures on 25 January are higher inside the main oval with a cold region (T about 650 K) outside the main oval at longitudes 240°–330°. Please better describe this part or rephrase.

In Figure 3a and 3d, the authors show the temperature maps obtained in the two dates. It is quite intriguing the fact that temperature is maximum inside the main oval and in the longitude region 90°–240° on 25th January, while on 14th April the maximum temperature value is outside the main oval and at 270°–300° longitude. A different behavior seems to occur on the Southern hemisphere during the same date, where there is a hot region at about 150°. It would be interesting to discuss in the text these differences among the two dates.

Figure 6 (extended data Figure 3) shows the $H3^+$ temperature as a function of latitude obtained during the two nights of observations. Although it is clear that on 25th January the retrieved temperature is higher than on 14th April for latitudes of 45° equatorward, error bars are missing and so it is not completely evident if the difference is significant. Another possibility would be showing the temperature difference, associated with the error bars superposed to the temperature. This would help in immediately catching the amount of temperature difference.

(Adapted from "Global upper-atmospheric heating on Jupiter by the polar aurorae" by O'Donoghue, J., Moore, L. & Bhakyapaibul, T. in *Nature*, Vol. 596, 2021.)

Questions:

1. What is the reviewer's attitude toward this paper? How can you tell it from the comments?

2. The first paragraph is a summary of the reviewed paper. According to the given excerpt, how can we organize a peer review?

3. Reviewers are supposed to remain factual and provide helpful suggestions. Has the reviewer followed these principles? How can you tell it from the excerpt? Discuss the two questions with your classmates and share ideas with one another.

4. Submitted papers should contain sufficient new insights to warrant a publication. Did the authors present any new insight? What is it?

Passage B

Referee #2 (Remarks to the Author):

This manuscript is generally well written and presented; however, there are many instances of language that overstates the data (or over simplifies it). There is a lack of clarifying details in the main text for some of the major points in the paper (centromere structure and evolution) that, when filtered out through the supplemental data and referenced works, render some conclusions overstated with the data in hand.

I highlight below some major comments with respect to comments above, as well as minor comments that would improve the manuscript. Overall, this reviewer is left to wonder why the focus of this paper centers on the centromere, with limited data to support some of the claims made, rather than highlighting other parts of the chromosome in more detail.

Line 44—In the abstract, the authors state that they "complete the orthologous chromosome 8 centromeric regions in chimpanzee, orangutan, and macaque for the first time" but later in the paper they highlight that these are "draft assemblies" (line 368).

Lines 93–94—The sentence wording here makes it unclear to the reader why the ONT reads harbor more sequence variation (i.e. they are longer).

Line 109—The wording in the main text is not abundantly clear on whether the primary assembly from Nurk and colleagues was the foundation for this improvement or if a complete reassembly occurred. If this is an improvement, the authors should describe how this improved the Nurk et al. assembly (contig reduction, correction, etc.) with respect to this previous chr8 assembly.

Lines 139–140 and 151–154—These statements as worded are confusing. In this region of the new assembly, the authors were able to "resolve one of the largest common inversion polymorphisms in the human genome (3.89 Mbp in length)", which is indicated in Fig 1c. Where is this in relation to the 4.56 Mbp region in the GRCh38 assembly? It is implied that the additional sequence added to this locus to build a 7.06 Mbp locus that includes this 3.89 Mbp region but where in this sequence with respect to GRCh38 is not clear—a comparison to GRCh38 in the figure would help. How much of the new assembly included this 3.89 inversion or does the new assembly add more information to the surrounding regions allowing for better resolution of the breakpoints? The wording of this sentence is vague in terms of whether CHM13 actually carries the inversion with respect to GRCh38 or if this description refers to the fact there is a polymorphic inversion that can be found in some human genomes at this location. In the last sentence of this paragraph the authors state that resolution of the alternate haplotype is important since the inverted haplotype predisposes to various human disorders, but again, is the inversion found in CHM13? The wording of this section is not explicitly clear. In Figure 1d, the data that was used to determine copy number polymorphisms in the human population should be referenced.

(Adapted from "The structure, function and evolution of a complete human chromosome 8" by Logsdon, G. A., Vollger, M. R., Hsieh, P. et al. in *Nature*, Vol. 593, 2021.)

 Questions:

1. According to the reviewer, what is the problem with the data and how should the author resolve the problem?
2. In the review, the misuse of wording has caused many problems. Can you point out some of them?
3. In a paper, the content must be innovative and improve the state of the art. Also both the applied methodology and evaluation method need to be sound and rigorous. In addition, the paper must be well structured and linguistically correct to adequately convey its content to readers. Can you judge from the review whether this paper has achieved the above requirements? Discuss with your classmates and share ideas with one another.

Part V
Reading for Writing

Peer review plays an important role in polishing a paper. Please read Passage A in "Reading for Speaking" and write a small article with no less than 200 words that answers the following questions:

- What problems does the reviewer point out?
- If you were the submitting author, how would you respond to the problems?
- After reading the review, could you please summarize what an excellent paper should be like?

Exercises

I. **Write a review for the following English abstract according to the structure and criteria you have learned in this unit (the Chinese abstract is just for your reference).**

Abstract

Objective: To investigate the CT, MRI and PET/CT imaging features of lymphoepithelioid cyst of the pancreas (LEC). **Materials and Methods:** 15 cases of pathologically confirmed LEC from December 2011 to May 2018 were included and their CT, MRI and PET/CT imaging features were retrospectively analyzed by two experienced doctors. **Results:** 3 lesions were located in the body, 2 in the body and tail and 10 in the tail. The lesions had a tendency of high tension and exogenous growth. They were single or multiple low to isodense cystic lesions without pancreatic duct dilatation. The cystic wall was often with tiny spot calcification but no nodules. The average maximum diameter was about 42.8mm. MR showed low T1WI, high signal on T2WI and high signal on DWI. With the increase of B value, the DWI signal intensity of lesions decreased. The ADC value did not decrease significantly. On dynamic contrast enhancement scan the intracystic components of the lesion were not enhanced, and the wall and septum of the lesion were gradually enhanced, which was higher than that of the surrounding normal pancreatic tissue. All the lesions showed no uptake on the 18F-FDG PET/CT examination. **Conclusion:** The imaging of pancreatic LEC has certain characteristics, which is helpful to the diagnosis of the disease.

Keywords: Cysts; Lymphoepithelial; Pancreas; Computed Tomography; Magnetic resonance imaging

胰腺淋巴上皮囊肿影像学表现分析

【摘要】**目的：**探讨胰腺淋巴上皮囊肿（LEC）的 CT、MRI 及 PET/CT 影像学表现，以提高对本病的认识。**资料与方法：**回顾性分析 2011 年 12 月至 2018 年 5 月间于本院经手术切除及病理学证实的 15 例 LEC 患者资料，并由 2 名医师分析患者术前的 MR、CT 及 PET/CT 影像资料。**结果：**3 例病变位于体部，2 例位于体尾部，10 例位于尾部。病灶具有高张力、外生性生长趋势，不伴胰管扩张的单或多囊状，低至等密度囊性灶，囊壁多伴微小点状钙化，不伴壁结节，平均最大径约 42.8mm。MR 上表现为 T1WI 低信号（较自由水 / 胆囊信号高），T2WI 高信号（较自由水 / 胆囊信号低），DWI 呈高信号，随 B 值增高，病灶信号强度减低，ADC 值无明显减低。增强后病灶囊内成分无强化，囊壁及分隔出现渐进性强化，高于周围正常胰腺组织。病灶无糖代谢增高。**结论：**胰腺淋巴上皮囊肿的影像学表现具有一定的特征，有助于疾病的诊断。

【关键词】胰腺肿瘤；淋巴上皮囊肿；计算机体层成像；磁共振成像

II. There are two reviewers commenting on the same paper. Read the peer reviews and then complete the exercises.

Reviewer #1 (Remarks to the Author):

This manuscript studies the future trends and opportunities for the decarbonization of China's power system through renewable energy and energy storage, with four scenarios considered, including 1) business as usual scenario (BAU), 2) Low-cost renewables scenario (R), 3) Carbon constraints scenario (C50), and 4) Deep carbon constraints scenario (C80). The topic is interesting. However, this paper ***entails*** notable ***technical defects*** as follows. Therefore, it is recommended not to accept this manuscript ***in the current form***.

Detailed comments:

1. This paper lacks a detailed literature review on the renewable potentials, current profile, relevant research methods, which are referred to for this study.

2. The section "Mix of generation capacities and power generation" presents some ***arbitrary data*** and information without scientific reasoning and process. The authors should present a ***scientific procedure*** with the methodology explained in detail. Based on the procedure, methodology and data used, then the author can explain the results and findings.

3. This paper also ***lacks specific information*** regarding the potentials and requirements for each type of renewable energy sources, e.g., the installation of wind turbines need to ***meet certain requirements*** such as distance from cities and wind speed etc. Similarly, the utilization of nuclear is also stringently constrained. These constrains are not taken into account in this paper.

4. The writing style is far away from ***scientific writing***, e.g., what is the

supporting information, such as data or reference, for the following statement? ***The costs of*** solar photovoltaics (PV), wind, and battery storage have decreased rapidly approximately 65% to 85% since 2010 and are projected to decrease further in the near future.

5) The ***language is poor with grammar issues and typos***. The title should not be a sentence—use highlights and extracted words instead.

Reviewer #2 (Remarks to the Author):

I believe this study has the potential to be published since it ***brings novel results*** and can influence thinking in the field; however, some assumptions made by the authors when running the SWITCH-China model should be ***clarified***. Please find below my main comments.

Line 57. The authors affirm that PV, wind, and battery storage costs have decreased rapidly to approximately 65% to 85% since 2010. Please ***insert the references*** and present the assumptions behind those numbers.

Line 71. Please clarify the main assumptions considered during the update process. Moreover, this study is based on the SWITCH-China model (reference #10), whose structure is not familiar to everybody. It is not quite clear the difference between this study and the modeling effort within reference #10. A brief description of the updates and an additional explanation about the basic technical assumptions of the model could also be provided in the supplementary material.

Lines 95–108. The presented results ***make sense*** under the statements of the paper. The fact that the cost of renewables would constantly decrease explains the increasing share of renewables in the energy matrix. However, it lacks a better explanation of how and why the different energy sources increase/decrease their participation in the capacity mix for the four scenarios. In my opinion, the results are too descriptive and lack ***technical discussion***, even if a very brief one. For example, take one type of renewable source (PV, for instance) and then briefly describe which kind of technology evolution ***justifies*** an increasing share of this type of renewable source in China's electricity matrix. Does the model consider private and government investment capacities over the next 10 years? As you know, wind and solar power plants are related to very high CAPEX per installed MW.

The fact that the future OPEX (mainly fuel cost) is reduced in BAU and R scenarios does not necessarily mean that these savings in brownfield plants would be promptly available to be invested in new greenfield projects. Please clarify how the SWITCH-China model ***deals with*** possible ***limitations*** in investment capacity until 2030.

Line 101. Typos: "inceasying", "capcities", "storage cpcities".

Lines 141–151. The discussion in chart 5a and 5b makes total sense, however, it lacks some technical explanation on the assumptions behind the emission and cost reduction curves.

Lines 151–156. Please clarify in the manuscript what the cost of conserved CO_2 means, especially when it is negative. What is the reference basis (in terms of energy source) to account for the avoided carbon in China?

Figure 9. Something is wrong with the subtitles.

Line 375. Is not the assumption of 1% of the capital costs with O&M costs for renewable energy too low? Please cite one or more references that give support to this assumption.

(Adapted from peer review of "Rapid cost decrease of renewables and storage accelerates the decarbonization of China's power system" by He, G., Lin, J., Sifuentes, F., Liu, X., Abhyankar, N. & Phadke, A. in *Nature Communication*, Vol. 11, 2020.)

1. **Fill in the blanks with the italicized words or expressions from the reviews above. Change the form if necessary.**

1) The results ________ with adequate ________.

2) More details about the true potential and ________ of the presented approach beyond human would make this study more attractive or a broader audience.

3) It then briefly describe which kind of technology evolution ________ an increasing share of this type of renewable source in China's electricity matrix.

4) Whether this correlates with protection from hospitalization, which is the key parameter, is not clear and is ________ by this report.

5) This paper ________ a detailed literature review on the renewable potentials,

current profile, relevant research methods, which are referred to for this study.

6) Since the data is ________ and the scientific reasoning is inadequate, i suggest not to accept this paper ________.

2. **Answer the following questions according to the text above.**

1) According to reviewer 1, what should the authors do with the data and references in their paper?

2) According to reviewer 2, what are the problems about the assumptions the authors have made?

3) Summarize the two reviewers' comments on the paper's problems. Try to find out their similarities and differences.

3. **Based on the two peer reviews, sum up the advantages and disadvantages of the paper and give some suggestions for improvement.**

	Advantages of the paper	Disadvantages of the paper	Suggestions
Reviewer 1			
Reviewer 2			

III. Read the following passage and complete the exercises.

A scientific paper is a good scientific paper for several reasons. In general, a reviewer gives an overview of the strong and weak points of a paper. First and foremost, the content must be innovative and improve the state of the art, but also both the applied methodology and evaluation method need to be sound and rigorous. (1) ________, the paper must be well structured and linguistically correct to adequately convey its content to readers. Consequently, a good reviewer should pay attention to all these aspects (and more) to produce a thorough review.

1) ______________________

A title should adequately "flag" the content of the paper. Although a title may be catchy, a scientific paper is not a newspaper article. A potentially interested scholar wants to decide from the title whether or not he/she spends time on reading the paper. Also, most of the search engines display paper titles in their result list. Hence, the precise wording used in the title is very important and deserves proper attention and thinking.

An abstract functions roughly similarly to a title, but with more lines of text. Some journals impose a fixed structure for the abstract (purpose, problem, method, material, and results) and usually limit it to a maximum number of words. A good abstract is a stand-alone summary of the paper. All the core elements of a paper should be included somehow. Abstracts are not a mere preliminary introduction or a repackaged conclusion section. As an abstract is a section on its own, it must be a self-containing text (no abbreviations, no references, no URLs, no undefined concepts, etc.) with its internal (2) _______ or flow of thought. Less adequate abstracts are a concatenation of copied/pasted phrases from all over the paper. Again, an abstract is best judged after a reviewer has read the entire paper.

2) ______________________

Another frequently used general criterion to be evaluated is the importance of the research questions or, alternatively, the potential impact of the work. As this criterion is more of a speculative and subjective nature, it can sometimes be difficult to provide an objective and substantiated answer. A well-written paper with a sound methodology can be "killed" if considered as (3) _______ relevant to the field or having only a superficial potential impact. In essence, a negative comment on this criterion to authors could mean that they have spent a considerable amount of their research time on futilities. Reviewers should thus formulate a negative opinion on this criterion in a cautious way backed up by references underpinning this opinion.

3) ______________________

A detailed description of the hypotheses of the evaluation, benchmarks, baseline approaches, gold standards, evaluation methods, procedures, and analysis of the observed results is required. Statistical methods should be used to ensure (4) _______, significance, and generality of the reported experimental results. Further, a good reviewer must be prepared to not only evaluate positive results but also results that falsify the hypotheses, i.e., negative results.

4) ____________________

Usually, results lead to new avenues for future research. Papers without some statements (sometimes in the conclusions section) on future work, lack ambition and point to an insufficiently elaborated paper. Reviewers have to challenge authors for their new ideas resulting from their current work. Kind reviewers might even give some suggestions for future work themselves, although authors cannot expect this to be a standard attitude by reviewers as the latter cannot be credited for it (or only anonymously).

A conclusion summarizes what authors consider to be their most important messages of the entire paper, not necessarily only of the results obtained. A reviewer should carefully examine whether the conclusions put forward are really substantiated by the paper. Conclusions echo the statements made in the (5) ________ as the conclusion section is supposed to summarize the "answers" to the research questions and challenges mentioned in the introductory section.

5) ____________________

A good list of bibliographic references complies with several criteria. It contains references to the most relevant related work and state of the art at the time of writing. The references are complete (full name of the source and page numbers), correct (no typos in the names), and appropriately formatted (according to the style guide). As a reviewer, you should check whether the bibliography represents a good mix of older and more recent work. References to very general textbooks rather than to thematically focused publications can point not only to a very new topic or area but also to authors who are new to a domain or unaware of previous work done. The same goes for a list of only or majorly recent references. (6) ________ self-referencing cannot be excluded (as every researcher builds on his/her previous work), authors should not exaggerate, as it can also be a sign of a researcher working in isolation without considering related work in his/her area. It should be clear that reviewers themselves have to be seasoned researchers in their domain and well (7) ________ of the latest work by peers and new trends in their field.

6) ____________________

It is delicate for a reviewer, in particular as a nonnative speaker, to make remarks on language and style errors. (8) ________, fuzzy language obfuscates the messages an author wants to convey. Authors should make use of available spell and style checking tools. A reviewer should not do all the language/stylistic corrections for the authors. But reviewers cannot simply overlook (evident) linguistic and stylistic problems and have to point out sentences that are difficult or ambiguous to understand. This evidently also applies to review comments.

7) ____________________

It is very common to find tables or some other way to schematically organize data in papers, in particular in discussion or evaluation sections. Reviewers should not simply take for granted the interpretations or explanations authors attribute to data. It happens regularly that authors overgeneralize trends, "stretch" how they interpret (9) ________ to support their theory, or simply draw a wrong conclusion. It is good reviewer practice to scrupulously verify that statements made by authors are really justified by the data. Structuring the data in a visually supportive way to guide a reader toward the statement(s) or conclusion(s) proposed by authors can be helpful but at the same time misleading. Reviewers have to ponder whether the data presented is complete. It is possible that these kinds of reflections point to weaknesses or overlooked angles of a (complex) research question. It is the job of a reviewer to consider such issues.

8) ____________________

Authors often make use of statistics to prove the validity of results. For example, user studies or evaluations involving a reference or gold standard usually calculate whether or not results (e.g., similar behavior of two setups) are due to chance and which level of significance the results have. Statistics, as formalizations, increase the perception of (10) ________ and seriousness of the work, allowing for the generalization of the results. However, depending on the exact setup of the experiments, different statistical tests apply. Reviewers should therefore examine if the statistical tests that the authors apply are indeed the correct ones and whether or not the authors correctly accept or reject the initial hypotheses.

Innovativeness

Innovativeness or originality of the work is a popular criterion in paper (and proposal) reviews. On the one hand, this can create an inflation of so-called news claims, buzzwords, or techniques without existing ones being properly or exhaustively researched or verified/falsified. (11) _______, submitted papers should contain a sufficient amount of new insights to warrant a publication. Conference chairs or journal editors usually include in the review instructions how strong the focus on innovativeness is.

(Adapted from *Scientific Peer Reviewing: Practical Hints and Best Practices* by Spyns, P. & Vidal, M., New York: Springer, 2015.)

1. Read the passage and match each section with the right subtitle.

1) ____________________ Language and Style

2) ____________________ Tables/Data

3) ____________________ Evaluation Methodology

4) ____________________ Title and Abstract

5) ____________________ Quality of Bibliography

6) ____________________ Research Questions and Potential Impact

7) ____________________ Statistics

8) ____________________ Future Directions and Valid Conclusions

2. Read the passage and fill in the blanks with the appropriate expressions you think fit.

aware	data	logic	on the other hand
introduction	in addition	although	reproducibility
nevertheless	marginally	solidity	

3. **Judge whether the statements are true or false according to the above passage about peer review.**

	Descriptions about peer review	True	False
1	The title in scientific papers should be as catchy as possible to interest scholars though they are not so precise.		
2	An abstract should include all the core elements of a paper.		
3	A well-written paper with a sound methodology will be definitely published.		
4	Reviewers evaluate positive results but ignore results that falsify the hypotheses.		
5	Statements on future work are not required to be included in papers.		
6	Research questions ought to be answered in conclusion section.		
7	The newest bibliographic references are the best for consultation.		
8	Language or style problems will be corrected by reviewers or editors.		
9	Authors sometimes over-interpret date and draw a wrong conclusion.		
10	Whether the statistical tests that the authors apply are correct will be examined by reviewers before publication.		

Project

Work in groups. You need to:

1. Collect 5 MA theses written by Chinese students in English.
2. Work separately as reviewers of the MA theses. Evaluate them according to the checklist below.
3. Discuss in groups the major problems of the theses you agree on.
4. Prepare a report for presentation in class.

Checklist for examining a paper				
	Items	Yes	No	Not necessary
1	**Introduction**			
	Expose the nature of the problem with insight.			
	Check carefully the relevant bibliography, with the purpose of guiding the reader.			
	Select the method.			
	Mention the principal results of the survey.			
	Define the principal conclusions suggested by the results.			
2	**Literature Review**			
	Summarize existing research to answer a review question.			
	Identify important gaps in the existing body of literature.			
	Provide the context for new research.			
3	**Method and Results**			
	The research and the results present a significant new advance to a clearly identified technological problem or scientific question.			
	The experimental methods are appropriate, and they are described clearly and with sufficient details for the work to be repeatable.			
	Be short and objective without verbosity.			
	The data need to be presented simply and clearly, since they represent new knowledge emerging in the world.			
	Avoid repeating others' results in words.			
4	**Results and Discussion**			
	Avoid redundancy.			
	The paper results are to be explained and commented upon, but never summed up.			

(continued)

Checklist for examining a paper				
Items		Yes	No	Not necessary
	Reveal the theoretical consequences and the possible practical applications of their researches.			
5	**Wording/Style**			
	Use correct tense; the materials and methods and the results sections should be in the past tense, much of the discussion in the present tense.			
	Adopt academic expressions.			
	Utilize well-structured/logical order.			
	Do not use hyperbole.